Summer 2000 Edition

COLLECTOR'S VALUE GUIDE™

Ty® Beanie Babies®

Collector Handbook and Price Guide

NINTH EDITION

Ty® Beanie Babies®

Front cover (left to right, from top): "Curly™" (*Beanie Kids™*); "The Beginning™" (*Beanie Babies®*); "Fleecie™" (*Beanie Babies®*); "2000 Signature Bear™" (*Beanie Babies®*); Rascal™" (*Beanie Kids™*).

Back cover (left to right): "Angel™" (*Beanie Kids™*); "Sneaky™" (*Beanie Babies®*); "Hippie™" (*Beanie Buddies®*); "Pinky™" and "Glory™" (*Teenie Beanie Babies™*).

Managing Editor:	Jeff Mahony	Creative Director:	Joe T. Nguyen
Associate Editors:	Melissa A. Bennett	Production Supervisor:	Scott Sierakowski
	Jan Cronan	Senior Graphic Designers:	Lance Doyle
	Gia C. Manalio		Susannah C. Judd
	Paula Stuckart		David S. Maloney
Contributing Editor:	Mike Micciulla		Carole Mattia-Slater
Editorial Assistants:	Timothy R. Affleck	Graphic Designers:	Jennifer J. Bennett
	Heather N. Carreiro		Sean-Ryan Dudley
	Jennifer Filipek		Kimberly Eastman
	Beth Hackett		Marla B. Gladstone
	Nicole LeGard Lenderking		Robert Kyerematen
	Steven Shinkaruk		Angi Shearstone
	Joan C. Wheal		David Ten Eyck
Web Reporter:	Samantha Bouffard	Art Interns:	Huy Hoang
			Anna Zagajewska
		Web Graphic Designer:	Ryan Falis
		Product Development Manager:	Paul Rasid
		R&D Specialist:	Priscilla Berthiaume

ISBN 1-888-914-87-4

CheckerBee PUBLISHING

306 Industrial Park Road
Middletown, CT 06457

www.collectorbee.com

TABLE OF CONTENTS

COLLECTOR'S
VALUE GUIDE™

INTRODUCING THE COLLECTOR'S VALUE GUIDE™

Welcome to the Summer 2000 Collector's Value Guide™ to Ty® Beanie Babies®. Now in its ninth edition, the Collector's Value Guide™ remains your essential source for new and exciting information about *Beanie Babies, Beanie Buddies®, Teenie Beanie Babies™* and the new *Beanie Kids™*!

Welcome!

The Collector's Value Guide™ also provides everything you need to catalog and keep track of your collection. In addition to issue and retirement dates, you'll find up-to-date market values for each tag generation. And that's not all. Find out how to discover variations in your collection, then check out the top ten most valuable *Beanie Babies* to see if you're the lucky owner of any of these sought-after pieces! Other great features inside these pages include:

- A close-up look at the nine new Beanie Kids, as well as the newest Beanie Babies and Beanie Buddies

- **A detailed guide on how to determine which swing tag and tush tag your Beanie has, including the new 6th generation Beanie Babies tag**

- Fun stories about Beanie Babies who have made headlines

- **A spotlight on the other Ty products**

- A guide on how to spot counterfeit Beanies

- **Information on how to search the secondary market from the comfort of your own home**

- And so much more!

THE BEANIE BABIES®
STORY

It may seem as if *Beanie Babies* have been here forever, but they actually made their first appearance in 1993. That was the year that the "Original Nine" *Beanie Babies* made their debut at a Chicago-area trade show. The following year, those nine critters appeared on the shelves of small gift and specialty shops nationwide, where they waited to be taken to a loving home, never dreaming that they would soon be part of a nationwide craze that would help Ty Inc. become the most lucrative toy company in the world.

Welcome To Chicago!

BROUGHT TO YOU BY . . .

Beanie Babies are the brainstorm of H. Ty Warner, a self-made billionaire who got his start in the plush toy business by working as a sales representative for the stuffed animal manufacturer Dakin Inc. Warner made a reputation for himself early on, when he would meet his clients dressed in a fur coat and top hat and driving a Rolls Royce. In the early 1980s, Warner quit his job at Dakin to travel overseas, returning to the United States in 1986. It was at that time he launched his own plush toy company, Ty Inc., with a small line of stuffed Himalayan cats and a few dogs. Warner's reputation and business quickly grew, and before long Ty Inc. had quite a successful menagerie on its hands!

None of Warner's previous successes could begin to compare with the wild enthusiasm that *Beanie Babies* provoked. Warner launched the *Beanie Babies* line with the intention of providing kids with a plush product that they could buy with their allowances. Little did he know that teens and adults would be just as captivated by his cuddly critters. As word of mouth about the purposely under-stuffed animals spread, so did the momentum.

Because Ty favors quality over quantity, *Beanie Babies* are not sold to large chain stores, but to smaller specialty stores that have a restriction on how many *Beanies* they can order at any given time. Consequently, as the demand for *Beanies* increased, they became more and more difficult to find. In the early *Beanie* years, it wasn't uncommon for gift shops to post signs on their doors reading "We are sold out of *Beanie Babies*" in order to ward off the inevitable question from hopeful customers.

In early 1995, Ty Inc. added fuel to the fire when it retired three of the early *Beanie Babies*. The hunt was on as collectors suddenly had to have them! As more *Beanie Babies* headed for a life of retirement, a secondary market opened up in which people were willing to pay large sums of money to own a rare or retired *Beanie*. Also, with large groups of *Beanies* being introduced and retired twice a year, people began asking Ty for a way to track that information. In 1996, Ty granted their wish, unveiling an official web site, *www.ty.com*. By 1999, the site had been visited over 3 billion times!

BEANIES ON THE SOCIAL SCENE

By 1997, the popularity of *Beanie Babies* had reached such a peak that Ty Inc. was asked to sponsor promotional giveaways at professional sporting events. The Chicago Cubs were the first team to host a *Beanie Baby* giveaway night, with Ty Warner throwing out the opening pitch! The event was such a grand-slam success that more than 50 Major League Baseball promotions have been held since then. The NBA, WNBA, NFL and NHL have all gotten into the spirit, holding successful promotions of their own.

The success of *Beanies* became even more evident when, that same year, Ty Inc. and McDonald's teamed up for a promotion. McDonald's offered a smaller version of *Beanie Babies*, called *Teenie Beanie Babies*, in its Happy Meals. Collectors lined up early to receive their adorable toys, which came in their own special bags. The promotion, originally slated to run for more than a month, ended after just two weeks due to the overwhelming demand and rapidly dwindling supply. *Teenie Beenie Babies*, along with just about everything else from the promotion, have now gained value on the secondary market. McDonald's and Ty teamed up again in 1998 and 1999, and fans were only too happy to add more *Teenie Beanies* to their collections, including *Teenie Beanie* versions of "Maple" and "Britannia," whose full-sized counterparts had only been available in Canada and Great Britain, respectively. Another promotion slated for 2000 is sure to bring just as much excitement to loyal collectors.

The year 1997 also marked the first time that a *Beanie Baby* was officially used to benefit a charity. On October 29, 1997, "Princess" was released in memory of the recently deceased Diana, Princess of Wales. All proceeds from the sale of "Princess" were donated to the Diana, Princess of Wales Memorial Fund. The purple bear, especially the earlier version made with P.V.C. pellets, was wildly popular and difficult to find. Two years later, "Princess" the *Beanie Buddy* made her debut, with proceeds from her sales also donated to the charity.

THE BUDDY SYSTEM

By the end of 1997, it would have been easy for Warner to rest on his laurels. After all, *Beanie Baby* collecting had become a national obsession, one that was spreading overseas to Great Britain and north to Canada, as well. But Warner, a master of marketing and publicity, still had more tricks up his sleeve. In 1998, the *Beanie Buddies* – larger, mirror-images of *Beanie Babies* – were introduced. Made from an exclusive material called Tylon®, *Beanie Buddies* are extremely soft and cool to the touch. The production process of Tylon® is slow, which keeps the availability of the *Buddies* limited and creates an even higher demand.

The *Buddies* collection continues to grow in popularity (and size), as 31 new *Buddies* – including large, extra large and jumbo sizes – were released in early 2000.

CLUBBY® COMES TO TOWN

Other big news in 1998 included the debut of the Beanie Babies® Official Club™ (BBOC™), which was launched by Ty in conjunction with Cyrk Inc. The club offered members a special Gold Kit, the opportunity to purchase an exclusive "Clubby" *Beanie Baby*, access to special web site pages and breaking *Beanie Babies* news. In 1999, a new Platinum Edition club kit was released that came with the *Beanie Baby* "Clubby II." The kits also included a newsletter, advising of opportunities to send away for future club pieces. This included the *Beanie Buddy* "Clubby," available to anyone who purchased the Gold charter kit; and the *Beanie Buddy* "Clubby II," available for collectors who had purchased either the Gold or the Platinum kit. As of this year, the BBOC has not introduced a new edition club kit. But collectors know that Ty always has something in store just around the corner.

COLLECTORS SHOW THEIR SUPPORT

There was no year more exciting for *Beanie Babies* fans than 1999. As the *Beanie Babies* line expanded to Japan, collectors were stunned by the August 31 announcement that all *Beanies* would retire as of December 31, 1999. This pronouncement fueled both panic and gossip, as collectors around the world tried to figure out if this really meant the end of *Beanie Babies*. The plot thickened when a statement appeared on the Ty web site that read,

"A very important global news flash will be made on December 24, 1999. Expect the unexpected!!!" This news flash contained an astounding announcement – Ty would put the fate of *Beanie Babies* in collectors' hands. A global vote was conducted from December 31 to January 2. Each vote cost 50 cents and all proceeds from the voting were donated to the Elizabeth Glaser Pediatric AIDS Foundation, thus continuing the charitable tradition of Ty Inc. When all was said and done, 91% of the voters were in favor of continuing the *Beanie Babies* line, and after tripling the amount of donations made by voters, Ty Inc. made a $1 million donation to the Foundation.

TY GIVES BIRTH TO KIDS™!

The future of *Beanie Babies* secured, collectors waited anxiously to see what Ty would do next. But they didn't have to wait long. On January 5, a news flash on the Ty web site announced "The world premiere of the Beanie _ _ _ _ will be unveiled . . ." and listed several upcoming gift shows throughout the United States, Canada, Europe and Japan. Within a few days, nine *Beanie Kids* made their debut. With birthdays and poems, the *Kids* are sure to be a big hit among those familiar with the *Beanie* line, as well as among newcomers who will no doubt fall in love with the *Kids'* life-like eyes and adorable expressions.

Beanie fans were further satisfied when prototypes of 20 new *Beanie Babies* were revealed on February 13, 2000 at the New York Toy Fair. Although the new *Beanies* weren't available right away, *Beanie* collectors all know that patience is a virtue!

Luckily for collectors, *Beanies* continue to be made, and the *Beanie* family continues to grow. As *Beanie* fans delight in the latest offerings – including the release of "Sakura," the first-ever Japanese exclusive – they also know that more exciting surprises could be unveiled at any second, and they smile and wait, content in the knowledge that Ty Warner will always keep them guessing.

THE NEW RELEASES

Ty Inc. kicked off the 21st century with quite a bang, releasing 31 new *Beanie Buddies*, nine *Beanie Kids* and 20 *Beanie Babies* within the first three months of the new year! You'd better start saving your pennies because you're going to want them all!

BEANIE KIDS™

With her blond hair and flower print dress, "Angel" just floated down from Heaven to be your special friend!

Don't let that innocent smile fool you. "Boomer" has quite a reputation for getting into mischief!

Do you hate getting up in the morning? "Chipper" will bounce out of bed with enough energy for both of you!

"Curly" certainly lives up to her name. That darling red hair is her pride and joy!

A girl like "Cutie" certainly loves attention, and what collector wouldn't love to give her lots of it?

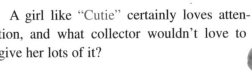

Despite her wild-looking red hair, "Ginger" is the sweetest spice in the cupboard!

Have you ever seen a gal quite as adorable as "Precious"? She gives new meaning to the phrase "pretty in pink."

Get ready to be amused, because "Rascal" loves the spotlight. He's ready to put on quite a show for you!

You'd better nail everything down when "Tumbles" comes over! This curious toddler gets into everything!

BEANIE BABIES®

The "2000 Signature Bear" has Ty's mark of approval visible right on its chest! The date 2000 and Ty's signature are both embroidered on this purple bear's red heart.

Even the spectacular Northern Lights are dimmed by the beauty of "Aurora." The North Pole shines a little brighter when this polar bear flashes a smile.

How did "Bushy" the lion get his name? Is it because of his bushy mane or bushy tail? Since "Roary" retired in 1998, there hasn't been a king of the Ty jungle, but this multicolored lion plans to change that!

"Fleecie" the lamb is as soft as fleece and sports a lavender bow around her neck. This is one little lamb you will want following you wherever you go!

"Frigid" the penguin's big, red beak and yellow tufts of hair are sure to warm the hearts of collectors from the North to the South Pole.

"Glow" the lightning bug has a smile on his face as he lights a way into your heart. He's the perfect companion for anyone afraid of the dark!

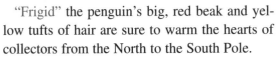

With paws clasped and eyes closed, "Grace" is praying you will take her into your home. This bunny is the perfect prayer companion for "Hope" the bear.

As long as "Halo II" is in your home, you will have a guardian angel nearby. Her puffy gold wings and distinct halo atop her head are absolutely heavenly!

Why is "Morrie" the eel so happy? His smile is positively electric! Maybe he's thinking about all the fun he'll have slithering among his new Ty friends.

"Niles" the camel is ready for a nap after traveling many miles from the hot desert to the Ty oasis. He's the second camel to join the Ty camp, following "Humphrey."

"Rufus" is a stylish dresser who proves that fashion has gone to the dogs. His brown bow perfectly matches the one big, brown spot on his back.

"Sarge" is sitting alert and ready to surprise his owner with an "attack" of hugs and licks. Once this playful pup gets you, you won't want him to let go!

There has never been a beetle quite as colorful as "Scurry." Made of several different colors – even some tie-dye – he is sure to scurry off store shelves as fast as his six legs can run!

It's been said that leopards don't change their spots, but with a name like "Sneaky," anything is possible. Keep your eye on this quick cat or he just might leave you in the dust!

"Springy" the lavender bunny is poised in mid-hop, ready to jump into your open arms. Could this happy hopper's name have anything to do with its leap year birth date?

"Swampy" usually spends his time in the misty marshes, but he has been known to poke his head out of the water to say "hello" to friends passing by.

"Swoop" the pterodactyl is ready to take flight with his vibrant blue-green wings. Just don't tell him that dinosaurs are supposed to be extinct!

If you thought "The End" was the last of the *Beanies*, "The Beginning" puts those fears to rest. Covered in holographic stars, this bear wants to be the "star" attraction of the new releases.

"Trumpet" is ready to signal his arrival with a toot from his tremendous trunk. This pleasant pachyderm will do anything for a peanut!

Although quite different in appearance from his fellow octopus, "Inky," a hug from "Wiggly" is just as tickly. With eight long tentacles perfect for hugging, you'll be pleasantly wrapped up!

BEANIE BUDDIES®

This purple bear, who proudly wears Ty Warner's signature, is all ready for the year 2000. Make sure you don't miss out on "2000 Signature Bear."

This tie-dyed dinosaur sure knows how to get with the times. "Bronty" is one brontosaurus who won't be going extinct anytime soon!

"Chocolate" is certainly a moose for collectors with a sweet tooth. So indulge yourself and take him home with you.

"Congo" has come a long way from his home in Africa to join other Buddy friends. Make sure you have plenty of bananas on hand for this hungry little ape!

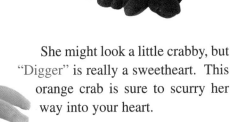

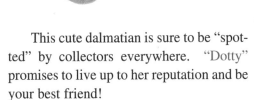

She might look a little crabby, but "Digger" is really a sweetheart. This orange crab is sure to scurry her way into your heart.

This cute dalmatian is sure to be "spotted" by collectors everywhere. "Dotty" promises to live up to her reputation and be your best friend!

"Dragon" is far from fierce. He's actually quite lovable and only breathes fire to warm your heart!

This huggable koala comes from "the land down under" where he snacks on his favorite leaves – "Eucalyptus" leaves, of course!

You'll "Flip" for the chance to own this adorable white kitty. Her sparkling blue eyes and pink ribbon make her the "cat's meow!"

"Flippity" is one of the few *Buddies* who doesn't have a *Beanie* counterpart. With his bright blue fur and his long, floppy ears, he's hard to resist!

Don't worry, this jelly fish does not sting. "Goochy" only uses his tentacles for swimming his way into your heart and offering hugs!

This hip bear sure is "Groovy" with his many pastel colors. Bring the retro movement into the 21st century by adding this *Beanie Buddy* to your collection!

"Hippie," "Large Hippie" and "Extra Large Hippie" are hip to the fact that bigger is better. These loveable bunnies are the perfect size for giving and receiving king-sized hugs!

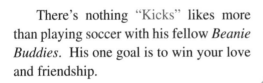

There's nothing "Kicks" likes more than playing soccer with his fellow *Beanie Buddies*. His one goal is to win your love and friendship.

"Large Fuzz" is one bear that definitely lives up to his name. Hugging his brown, fuzzy texture is like hugging a real bear cub – only much safer!

Give "peace" a chance by taking any one (or all!) of these three different-sized bears into your heart and home. But don't worry, "Large Peace," "Extra Large Peace" and "Jumbo Peace" won't eat you out of house and home – they are already stuffed!

This colorful tropical fish is sure to stand out in his school. Waiting for the right opportunity, "Lips" is anxious to give you a big kiss!

This lizard stayed out in the sun too long and turned a vibrant tie-dyed color. Now "Lizzy" turns the heads of all her *Buddies*.

"Lucky" the ladybug will want to "fly away home," especially if she is part of your family!

"Nanook" is taking a break from his dog sled-pulling chores by sitting next to you and being your new best friend.

"Osito" honors the United States' neighbor to the south by showing off the festive colors of Mexico's flag: green, white and red.

A chameleon of ever-changing pastel hues and shades, "Rainbow" hopes to blend into his environment – hopefully, with you!

Most turtles hide in their shells, but "Speedy" is not a reclusive reptile. He loves visiting his *Buddies,* even if it takes a while to get where he's going.

"Ty 2K" has arrived and is ready to celebrate the new millennium in style. His colorful coat of confetti fur is the life of any party!

"Valentino" doesn't wear his heart on his sleeve – he wears it on his chest! You won't be able to keep your hands off this cushy, soft favorite!

Dachshunds are honored with this version named "Weenie." With his droopy ears and sturdy legs, he is sure to steal your heart away!

Although "Zip" is royally regal in her black fur coat, scarlet ribbon, and pure white feet and muzzle, she'll always come looking for a hug and a squeeze from you!

EXCLUSIVE JAPANESE BEANIE BABY™

"Sakura" is the first Japanese exclusive from Ty! Her name means "cherry blossom," which is Japan's national flower.

HEADLINE NEWS

If it seems as though *Beanie Babies* are everywhere, that's because they are! Since their inception in 1994, *Beanie Babies* have made headlines around the country – and even the world! Here's a sampling of some standout news stories from the past and present that illustrate just how popular these bean bag critters are!

God Save the *Beanies*™

It appears that not even royalty is immune to the *Beanie Babies* craze. In February of 2000, 6-year-old Ryan Innes proudly presented Great Britain's Queen Elizabeth with "Scorch" the *Beanie Baby* when the Queen visited the Royal Air Force

Marham near Norfolk. Young Ryan graciously told the Queen that "Scorch" was his favorite, but then said she could keep it because he had another at home.

Beanie™ Drive-Through

What do a bank and a gift store have in common? A drive-through window! When the Tri-State Bean Bags store in Liberty Township, Ohio, opened for business in 1999 in a converted bank, its owner decided to keep the existing drive-through. Instead of money,

however, the window now serves *Beanies* to collectors on the go! While a store worker admits it's not the main source of *Beanie* withdrawals (most customers use the traditional front door), it does have a certain level of ambiance that the owner says will keep the window open "as long as Ty's in business."

On-Line Auction Fraud

Buyer beware! An Ohio woman and her two sons were recently charged with using Internet auction sites to sell counterfeit *Beanie Babies*. Meanwhile, in New Jersey, two men were charged with defrauding dozens of on-line customers by not shipping the *Beanie Babies* their customers had purchased. The lesson? Always be careful when buying *Beanie Babies* from Internet auction sites. You never know what you're getting, or in some cases, not getting.

Beanie Kids™ Mania

On February 12, 2000, excited collectors lined up in droves at 20 stores across the country that had been specifically selected by Ty Inc. to receive the first shipments of the new *Beanie Kids*. Most of the stores held raffles to determine the lucky few who would walk away clutching one of the prized *Kids*. One collector explained the appeal to the *Denver Post* saying, "It's the adrenaline rush. It's the thrill of it – being the first to buy before it gets on the shelf." Not long after this "super Saturday," *Beanie Kids* started popping up on various Internet auction sites, some selling for more than 10 times their retail value.

Beanie Babies® Unveiled

Ta-da! On February 13, 2000 at the American International Toy Fair held in New York City, 20 new *Beanie Baby* prototypes were unveiled before a crowd of retailers and toy industry insiders. While descriptions of the new *Beanie Babies* immediately flooded web sites devoted to the cuddly collectibles, the animals' names and photographs were not released to the public until March 1, 2000.

"Halo™" Lends A Helping Hand

When a fire tragically took the lives of six Massachusetts firefighters on December 3, 1999, residents of the Worcester community began a fund to help the families of the victims. Among other activities, a drive was started to collect "Halo" *Beanie Babies* to give to the families (especially the children) of the fallen firefighters, in hopes of offering them solace and comfort in their time of grieving. More than 70 "Halos" were collected from an amazing outpouring of support worldwide.

"Princess™" Update

Ty Inc. has an outstanding record of contribution to numerous charities, including the Diana, Princess of Wales Memorial Fund. All proceeds from the sales of "Princess" *Beanie Babies* and *Beanie Buddies* are donated to the fund, which carries on the late Princess' charitable works. On October 26, 1999, Ty Inc. Executive Vice President and Chief Financial Officer Michael W. Kanzler presented the Memorial Fund with a check for nearly $2 million, bringing the amount of Ty's contributions to more than $20 million in less than two years.

The Night The Lights Went Out In Ty® Land

Although collectors were forewarned that an important announcement would be taking place on the Ty web site on August 31, 1999, no one was prepared for the drama that would unfold. At midnight, *www.ty.com* went black and stayed that way until mid-afternoon when a news flash announced the introduction of new *Beanie Babies, Beanie Buddies,*

Attic Treasures and *Ty Plush (*now called *Ty Classic).* The excitement of the news was tempered by a shocking and cryptic message: "On December 31, 1999 . . . All *Beanies* will be retired . . . ." Although the announcement's presence on the web site was short-lived, the message sent shock waves throughout the *Beanie* world.

Teenie Beanies™ Success Not So Small

The popular McDonald's *Teenie Beanie Babies* promotions gained an added measure of fame in 1999 when the popular game show "Jeopardy" posed this Final Jeopardy query: "This most successful McDonald's promotion was run two times." Hmm, could the answer be "What is the *Teenie Beanie Babies* promotion, Alex?" Two more McDonald's promotions have been held since that "Jeopardy" episode aired; one offering 12 new *Teenie* companions, and a second that immediately followed and offered *Teenie Beanie Babies* International Bears. Another *Teenie Beanies* promotion is scheduled for June 2000, and McDonald's Europe began its second promotion in March 2000.

Heavy Hitters

Beanie Babies have infiltrated every aspect of American life – including sports. Along with the many *Beanie Babies* given away at national sporting events like baseball, basketball, football and hockey games, the plush critters have also received some high sporting honors. *The Sporting News* magazine named *Beanie Baby* "Glory" (who became a star himself at baseball's All-Star Game) one of the 100 most powerful people in sports for 1998. That same year, *Beanie Baby* "Valentino" got a place in the Baseball Hall of Fame in Cooperstown, New York, as part of the 1998 highlights exhibit. The reason? Valentino" was on hand as the promotional giveaway the night New York Yankees pitcher David Wells pitched a perfect game.

If you thought Ty Inc. only made *Beanie Babies,* you've got another think coming! When these darling bean bag animals first hit the collectibles market in 1994, Ty was already known for its adorable cuddly plush toys, which it still continues to make. Don't be surprised if that ordinary-looking teddy bear at your bedside turns out to be from the same amazing family as "#1 Bear," "Fuzz" and "Peanut!"

Ty Classic™ – Before bringing *Beanies* into the world, Ty Inc. created a line of stuffed plush animals, beginning in 1986. Originally called *Ty Plush,* the line consisted of dogs and cats for the pet lovers, and of course the favorite stuffed animal – bears! The line grew to include Country and Wildlife categories for such critters as raccoons, tigers and elephants – not exactly the type of pets you would expect to find strolling through your living room. This branch of the Ty family (which changed its name to *Ty Classic* in the year 2000) now numbers more than 380 items.

Attic Treasures™ – Have you ever seen an antique teddy bear? They used to be made with jointed limbs and a very dignified look. Well, in 1993, Ty began re-creating bears and hares just like that, harkening back the animals of yesteryear. And it must have been cold in that attic, because Ty eventually produced some of them with shirts, sweaters, overalls and hats. Some have even changed outfits from one year to the next! The collection was originally *The Attic Treasures Collection.* Shortly after its release, the line became *Ty Collectibles*, only to be changed back to its original name in 1998. This collection has grown into a family of more than 150 different creatures.

Pillow Pals® – A stuffed animal is one of those comforting things that appeal to anyone of any age. But in 1995 with the introduction of the *Pillow Pals* collection, Ty Inc. went out of its way to appeal to infants. This adorable menagerie is made up of all kinds of cuddly beasts, from dogs and frogs to hares and bears. At first, these animals were produced in muted, pastel shades, but in 1999 they began sporting bright eye-catching, neon colors. If you love cute animals designed to be as soft and cuddly as your favorite pillow, these *Pillow Pals* are for you! With more than 40 pieces to choose from, they're a sure winner. Where else can you see an orange koala, or a zebra with green stripes?

Baby Ty™ – The newest addition to the loveable Ty family is designed for the little ones, too. Released in January of 2000, the *Baby Ty* collection is made up of pastel-colored animals, similar to *Pillow Pals* but with a special secret – they each come with a rattle inside! With their beautiful colors and hidden rattle surprise, these six new animals are sure to be a big hit, especially with the youngest members of the family.

RECENT RETIREMENTS

In December of 1999, 51 *Beanie Babies* and 15 *Beanie Buddies* were retired. Here's an update of all the recent retirements, with each piece's stock number and issue year.

BEANIE BABIES®

Retired 12/23/99

1999 Holiday Teddy™
  (bear, #4257, 1999)
Almond™ (bear, #4246, 1999)
Amber™ (cat, #4243, 1999)
B.B. Bear™ (bear, #4253, 1999)
Beak™ (kiwi, #4211, 1998)
Butch™ (bull terrier, #4227, 1999)
Cheeks™ (baboon, #4250, 1999)
Chipper™ (chipmunk, #4259, 1999)
Early™ (robin, #4190, 1998)
Flitter™ (butterfly, #4255, 1999)
Fuzz™ (bear, #4237, 1999)
Germania™ (bear, #4236, 1999)
GiGi™ (poodle, #4191, 1998)
Goatee™ (mountain goat, #4235, 1999)
Goochy™ (jellyfish, #4230, 1999)
Groovy™ (bear, #4256, 1999)
Honks™ (goose, #4258, 1999)
Hope™ (bear, #4213, 1999)
Jabber™ (parrot, #4197, 1998)
Jake™ (mallard duck, #4199, 1998)
Kicks™ (bear, #4229, 1999)
Knuckles™ (pig, #4247, 1999)
KuKu™ (cockatoo, #4192, 1998)
Lips™ (fish, #4254, 1999)
Luke™ (black lab, #4214, 1999)

Retired 12/23/99, cont.

Mac™   (cardinal, #4225, 1999)
Mooch™ (spider monkey, #4224, 1999)
Neon™ (seahorse, #4239, 1999)
Paul™ (walrus, #4248, 1999)
Pecan™ (bear, #4251, 1999)
Prickles™ (hedgehog, #4220, 1999)
Roam™ (buffalo, #4209, 1998)
Rocket™ (blue jay, #4202, 1998)
Sammy™ (bear, #4215, 1999)
Scaly™ (lizard, #4263, 1999)
Scat™ (cat, #4231, 1999)
Schweetheart™
    (orangutan, #4252, 1999)
Scorch™ (dragon, #4210, 1998)
Sheets™ (ghost, #4260, 1999)
Silver™ (cat, #4242, 1999)
Slippery™ (seal, #4222, 1999)
Slowpoke™ (sloth, #4261, 1999)
Spangle™ (bear, #4245, 1999)
Swirly™ (snail, #4249, 1999)
The End™ (bear, #4265, 1999)
Tiny™ (chihuahua, #4234, 1999)
Ty 2K™ (bear, #4262, 1999)
Valentina™ (bear, #4233, 1999)
Wallace™ (bear, #4264, 1999)
Whisper™ (deer, #4194, 1998)

Retired 11/30/99

Osito™ (bear, #4244, 1999)

Retired 11/26/99

Tracker™
    (basset hound, #4198, 1998)

Retired 11/19/99

Halo™ (angel bear, #4208, 1998)

Retired 11/12/99

Millennium™ (bear, #4226, 1999)

Retired 10/27/99

Eucalyptus™ (koala, #4240, 1999)

Retired 10/25/99

1999 Signature Bear™
(bear, #4228, 1999)

Retired 10/21/99

Tiptoe™ (mouse, #4241, 1999)

Retired 7/30/99

Maple™ (bear, #4600, 1997)

BEANIE BUDDIES®

Retired 3/10/00

Fetch™
(golden retriever, #9338, 1999)

Retired 3/8/00

Ty 2K™ (bear, #9346, 2000)

Retired 2/10/00

Peanut™ (elephant, #9300, 1998)

Retired 1/31/00

Inch™ (inchworm, #9331, 1999)
Schweetheart™
(orangutan, #9330, 1999)

Retired 12/12/99

Chip™ (cat, #9318, 1999)
Gobbles™ (turkey, #9333, 1999)
Jabber™ (parrot, #9326, 1999)
Pinky™ (flamingo, #9316, 1999)
Rover™ (dog, #9305, 1998)
Snort™ (bull, #9311, 1999)
Snowboy™ (snowboy, #9342, 1999)
Spinner™ (spider, #9334, 1999)
Stretch™ (ostrich, #9303, 1998)
Waddle™ (penguin, #9314, 1999)

Retired 12/11/99

Bongo™ (monkey, #9312, 1999)
Hippity™ (bunny, #9324, 1999)
Humphrey™ (camel, #9307, 1998)

Retired 12/10/99

Jake™ (mallard duck, #9304, 1998)
Peking™ (panda, #9310, 1999)

Retired 11/29/99

Bubbles™ (fish, #9323, 1999)
Pumkin'™ (pumpkin, #9332, 1999)
Tracker™
(basset hound, #9319, 1999)

Retired 11/24/99

Chilly™ (polar bear, #9317, 1999)
Smoochy™ (frog, #9315, 1999)
Squealer™ (pig, #9313, 1999)

Retired 11/19/99

Erin™ (bear, #9309, 1999)
Millennium™ (bear, #9325, 1999)

Retired 11/17/99

Teddy™
(bear, #9306, 1998)

BEANIE BABIES® TOP TEN

Beanie Babies are still going strong on the secondary market. The pieces listed here have earned their place in the top ten rankings by being rare and/or limited (like variations or employee gifts) or early pieces with older generation tags.

#1 Bear™

Bear, Ty Sales Rep Gift
Market Value: Special Tag – $9,200

This bear certainly is aptly named! "#1 Bear" was distributed to the Ty Inc. sales representatives in December 1998 at a company sales conference at the Fairmont Hotel in Chicago. Only 253 of these bears were made. Ty Warner said he wanted to show his appreciation for his sales representatives who helped to make *Beanies* number one. The bear features a special hang tag with a dedication. Best of all, each one is hand-numbered and signed by Ty Warner himself!

Billionaire 2™

Bear, Ty Employee Gift
Market Value: Special Tag – $5,800

"Billionaire 2" was presented to Ty employees at a company picnic in Oak Brook, Illinois in September 1999. The soft fabric of "Billionaire 2" is similar to that of "Fuzz" and "Groovy." Only 475 of these special bears were made. Each tag is numbered and signed by Ty Warner, and features a special dedication. This rare bear is coveted by collectors everywhere.

Peanut™

Elephant, Dark Blue Version
Market Value: ❸ – $4,400

This extremely rare *Beanie Baby* was only available from June 1995 to October 1995 – just five months! When these dark blue elephants started shipping, the company realized a production error – "Peanut" was supposed to be light blue. The mistake was soon corrected, and for the next two and a half years, "Peanut" was only available in his light blue color. It is estimated that only 2,000 of the dark blue "Peanuts" were manufactured.

Teddy™ (violet)

Bear, Ty Employee Gift
Market Value: No Swing Tag – $3,800

"Teddy" (violet) is another Ty employee exclusive. This bear was given out in September 1996 at a Ty Inc. company party. This version sports the "new face" and a red ribbon, but has no swing tag. Only an estimated 300 to 400 of these "employee bears" were produced, making it a real challenge for collectors to add one to their collections.

Nana™

Monkey
Market Value: ❸ – $3,700

"Nana" was introduced in June of 1995; however, shortly after production began, this monkey's name was changed to "Bongo." While these two early versions appeared to be almost identical, not all "Nana" and "Bongo" *Beanie Babies* look alike. In February of 1996, "Bongo's" tail color changed to brown for five months, before reclaiming its (and "Nana's") original tan color.

Pinchers™

Lobster, "Punchers™" Swing Tag Version
Market Value: ❶ – $3,500

"Pinchers" was released in January of 1994 as one of the "Original Nine" *Beanie Babies*. This alone would make it a valuable piece, so add a tag error to the mix and you've got a top ten *Beanie*! When introduced in early 1994, this red lobster was produced briefly with a tag that said "Punchers." While some collectors believe this was the crustacean's original name, others maintain it was a typo. In any event, the switch in names has caused the value of this piece to skyrocket.

Brownie™

Bear
Market Value: ❶ – $3,200

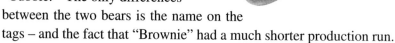

"Brownie" has the distinction of being one of the "Original Nine" *Beanie Babies* released in 1994. And making the bear even more valuable is the fact that after a relatively short time, his name became "Cubbie." The only differences between the two bears is the name on the tags – and the fact that "Brownie" had a much shorter production run.

Billionaire bear™

Bear, Ty Employee Gift
Market Value: Special Tag – $2,750

"Billionaire bear" was given to Ty employees on September 26, 1998 at the company's annual picnic. This bear was the first *Beanie Baby* to be manufactured with the super-soft Tylon® fabric, which was originally introduced on the *Beanie Buddies*. Each employee received two of these bears, which featured a special tag with a dedication that celebrated shipping over a billion dollars in merchandise since January of 1998 – and Ty Warner's signature. It is estimated that anywhere between 600 to 1,200 of these bears were produced.

Teddy™ (brown)

Bear, Old Face Version
Market Value: ❶ – $2,500

The six multi-colored (brown, cranberry, jade, magenta, teal and violet) "Teddys," which were originally released in 1994, are highly sought after by collectors. These bears were first released with old-fashioned Victorian-style faces that featured pointed snouts and eyes set far apart on the faces. In 1995, all the bears underwent cosmetic surgery and emerged with new faces that featured close-set eyes and rounded, lower snouts. Of all the "old face" bears, "Teddy" (brown) is the most desired.

Humphrey™

Camel
Market Value: ❶ – $2,450

When "Humphrey" the camel was first released in June of 1994, he was not a big hit with collectors. Perhaps the idea of a stuffed camel did not strike *Beanie* fans as being traditionally "cute;" however, collectors soon sought out the desert-dwelling darling. Humphrey's appeal became apparent after he became a member of the very first *Beanie Babies* retirement in 1995. Now collectors everywhere are scouring the globe, looking for "Humphrey!"

Ty® Swing Tags & Tush Tags

Every *Beanie* is manufactured with two tags – a swing tag and a tush tag. The swing tag, or hang tag, is a heart-shaped paper tag attached to the *Beanie* with a plastic connector. The tush tag is a small cloth tag attached to the *Beanie's* posterior.

Keeping your *Beanies'* tags intact and in mint condition is essential if you plan on re-selling them in the future. Removing the tags also removes most of the secondary market value. These tags are also important in determining secondary market value because, in most cases, the older *Beanies* are worth more. Usually the swing tag is the best indicator of the age of a piece because the year printed on the tush tag might not reflect the actual year in which the piece was made.

BEANIE BABIES® SWING TAGS

Generation ❶ (Early 1994 – Mid 1994): The first *Beanie Babies* came with red, heart-shaped, single-sheet swing tags. The "ty" logo on the front of the tag is printed in a skinny font, and both and logo and the outer edge of the heart are outlined in gold. The reverse side contains the animal's name and style number, as well as with the words "The Beanie Babies Collection" and relevant copyright and safety information.

The Beanie Babies Collection
Brownie ™ style 4010
© 1993 Ty Inc. Oakbrook, IL. USA
All Rights Reserved, Caution:
Remove this tag before giving
toy to a child. For ages 5 and up.
Handmade in Korea.
Surface
Wash.

Generation ❷ (Mid 1994 – Early 1995): The front of this tag looks identical to the first generation tag, but opens up like a book. Inside, the name of the collection, company information, care instructions and a cautionary warning are on the left, while the right side lists the *Beanie's* name and style number with the words "to ___ /from ____/with love."

The Beanie Babies Collection
© 1993 Ty Inc. Oakbrook IL. USA
All Rights Reserved, Caution:
Remove this tag before giving
toy to a child. For ages 3 and up.
Handmade in China
Surface
Wash.

Chilly ™ style 4012
to _____
from _____
with
love

Generation ❸ (Early 1995 – Early 1996): The "ty" logo is fatter and puffier than in previous versions. Inside, a trademark symbol now appears after the words "The Beanie Babies Collection," and the addresses of Ty's three corporate locations are listed.

> The Beanie Babies ™ Collection
> © Ty Inc.
> Oakbrook IL. U.S.A.
> © Ty UK Ltd.
> Waterlooville, Hants
> PO8 8HH
> © Ty Deutschland
> 90008 Nürnberg
> Handmade in China
>
> Garcia ™ style 4051
> to _____
> from _____
> with
> love

Generation ❹ (Early 1996 – Late 1997): Fourth generation tags look very different from previous versions. A yellow star containing the words "Original Beanie Baby" appears on the front of the tag in the upper right corner. The "ty" logo is no longer outlined in gold, and the "y" in "ty" is lower. Inside, the "to/from" section is replaced with the *Beanie's* birthday and poem, as well as the official Ty web site address.

> The Beanie Babies™Collection
> © Ty Inc.
> Oakbrook IL. U.S.A.
> © Ty UK Ltd.
> Fareham, Hants
> PO15 5TX
> © Ty Deutschland
> 90008 Nürnberg
> Handmade in China
>
> Doodle ™ style 4171
> DATE OF BIRTH : 3 - 8 - 96
> Listen closely to "cock-a-doodle-doo"
> What's the rooster saying to you?
> Hurry, wake up sleepy head
> We have lots to do, get out of bed!
> Visit our web page!!!
> http://www.ty.com

Generation ❺ (Late 1997 – Late 1999): In late 1997, a new generation tag appeared with the words "Original Beanie Baby" in a new typeface as well as changes to the inside text. The *Beanie's* birth date is written out, the words "Visit our web page" has been removed and the "http://" is no longer part of the web site address. The *Beanie's* style number is now part of the last four digits of the UPC bar code on the back of the tag. Finally, the phrase "The Beanie Babies Collection" is now registered, the trademark symbol has been dropped and the corporate offices overseas are referred to collectively as "Ty Europe."

> The Beanie Babies Collection®
> © Ty Inc.
> Oakbrook, IL. U.S.A.
> © Ty Europe Ltd.
> Fareham, Hants
> PO15 5TX, U.K
> © Ty Canada
> Aurora, Ontario
> Handmade in China
>
> Pinky™
> DATE OF BIRTH: February 13, 1995
> Pinky loves the everglades
> From the hottest pink she's made
> With floppy legs and big orange beak
> She's the Beanie that you seek!
> www.ty.com

In the summer of 1998, slight changes occurred. The writing inside the star logo is in a different font, and the writing on the inside and back of the tag is larger and darker. A few months later, the Ty Europe Ltd. address changed to "Gosport, Hampshire, U.K."

> The Beanie Babies Collection®
> © Ty Inc.
> Oakbrook, IL. U.S.A.
> © Ty Europe
> Gosport, Hampshire, U.K.
> © Ty Canada
> Aurora, Ontario
> Handmade in China

Generation 6 (Early 2000 – Current): On this swing tag, an iridescent silver star with a yellow "2000" replaces the familiar yellow star and the words "Original Beanie Baby." Inside is a listing of the Ty corporate locations: ©Ty Inc., ©Ty Canada, ©Ty Europe and ©Ty Japan.

The Beanie Babies Collection®
© Ty Inc.
© Ty Canada
© Ty Europe
© Ty Japan
Handmade in China

The Beginning™
DATE OF BIRTH: January 1, 2000
Beanie Babies can never end
They'll always be our special friends
Start the fun because we're here
To bring you hope, love and cheer!
www.ty.com

BEANIE BABIES® TUSH TAGS

Version 1: The first *Beanie Babies* tush tags were white on a horizontal layout, with production and company information in black ink.

© 1993 TY INC.
OAKBROOK IL, U.S.A.
ALL RIGHTS RESERVED
HAND MADE IN CHINA
SURFACE WASHABLE

ALL NEW MATERIAL
POLYESTER FIBER
& P.V.C. PELLETS
PA. REG #1965
FOR AGES 3 AND UP

Version 2: The first tag in a vertical layout contains the "ty" logo inside a red heart, and the information printed in red ink.

HAND MADE IN CHINA
© 1993 TY INC.,
OAKBROOK IL, U.S.A.
SURFACE WASHABLE
ALL NEW MATERIAL
POLYESTER FIBER &
P.V.C. PELLETS
REG. NO PA - 1965(KR)
FOR AGES 3 AND UP
CE

The Beanie Babies Collection™
Quackers
HAND MADE IN CHINA
© 1995 TY INC.
OAKBROOK IL, U.S.A.
SURFACE WASHABLE
ALL NEW MATERIAL
POLYESTER FIBER
& P.V.C. PELLETS CE
REG. NO PA. 1965(KR)

Version 3: On this tag, the phrase "The Beanie Babies Collection™" appears above the "ty" heart logo, and the animal's name is below the heart.

The Beanie Babies Collection™
★
Tuffy
HAND MADE IN CHINA
© 1996 TY INC.,
OAKBROOK IL, U.S.A.
SURFACE WASHABLE
ALL NEW MATERIAL
POLYESTER FIBER
& P.V.C. PELLETS CE
REG. NO PA. 1965(KR)

Version 4: This tag features a tiny red star on the upper left side of the "ty" heart logo. On some of the earliest versions, a clear sticker with the star is affixed next to the logo.

The Beanie Babies® Collection™
★
Hissy™
HAND MADE IN CHINA
© 1997 TY INC.,
OAKBROOK IL, U.S.A.
SURFACE WASHABLE
ALL NEW MATERIAL
POLYESTER FIBER
& P.V.C. PELLETS CE
REG. NO PA. 1965(KR)

Version 5: Beginning in late 1997, this version appeared with a registration mark after "Beanie Babies" in the collection's name, and a trademark symbol after the animal's name.

The Beanie Babies Collection®
★
Fetch™
HAND MADE IN CHINA
© 1998 TY INC.,
OAKBROOK IL, U.S.A.
SURFACE WASHABLE
ALL NEW MATERIAL
POLYESTER FIBER
& P.E. PELLETS CE
REG. NO PA. 1965(KR)

Version 6: The registration mark now appears after the word "Collection." Some of the tags note a change from "P.V.C." pellets to "P.E." In mid-1998, an oval red stamp containing numbers and Chinese characters began appearing inside some *Beanie Babies* tush tags.

COLLECTOR'S
VALUE GUIDE™

Version 7: On this tag, a hologram contains the name of the collection and two designs that can be seen depending on the angle from which the tag is viewed. Also, a red heart is printed on the tag in disappearing ink.

Millenium™
HANDMADE IN CHINA
© 1999 TY INC.,
OAKBROOK, IL. U.S.A.
SURFACE WASHABLE
ALL NEW MATERIAL
POLYESTER FIBER
& P.E. PELLETS CE
REG.NO PA. 1965(KR)

Honks™
HANDMADE IN CHINA
© 1999 TY INC.,
OAKBROOK, IL. U.S.A.
SURFACE WASHABLE
ALL NEW MATERIAL
POLYESTER FIBER
& P.E. PELLETS CE
REG.NO PA. 1965(KR)

Version 8: Beginning in the summer of 1999, the hologrammed tush tags began to appear as a single flap, unlike the previous tags, which were looped.

BEANIE BUDDIES® SWING TAGS

Generation ❶ (1998 - Late 1999): The front of the 1st generation *Beanie Buddies* tag resembles a *Beanie Babies* 5th generation swing tag (with the word "Buddy" replacing "Baby" inside the yellow star). Inside, on the right-hand side, the animal's name, a fact about its *Beanie Baby* counterpart and the official Ty web site address appear.

The Beanie Buddies Collection®
© Ty Inc.
Oakbrook, IL. U.S.A.
© Ty Europe Ltd.
Fareham, Hants
PO15 5TX, U.K.
© Ty Canada
Aurora, Ontario
Handmade in China

Rover™
Rover the BEANIE BABY
was the first non-breed dog.
Introduced in the summer of 1996
this red color set him apart!
www.ty.com

The Beanie Buddies Collection®
© Ty Inc.
Oakbrook, IL.
© Ty Europe
Gosport, Hamp
© Ty Canada
Aurora, Ontari
Handmade in Ch

The Beanie Buddies Collection®
© Ty Inc.
Oakbrook, IL. U.S.A
© Ty Europe
Gosport, Hampshire, U.K.
© Ty Canada
Aurora, Ontario
Handmade in China

The left side initially gave the Ty Europe Ltd. address as "Fareham, Hants." This was changed to "Gasport, Hampshire, U.K.," then later, the spelling was corrected to "Gosport, Hampshire, U.K."

Generation ❷ (Early 2000 - Current): The star on the front of the 2nd generation tag has been changed to pastel colors. Inside, the corporate addresses on the left-hand side of the tag has been changed to read "©Ty Inc., ©Ty Canada, ©Ty Europe and ©Ty Japan."

The Beanie Buddies Collection®
© Ty Inc.
© Ty Canada
© Ty Europe
© Ty Japan
Handmade in China

Flippity™
Flippity the BEANIE BABY
was never made. He is Flippity's missing twin !
www.ty.com

BEANIE BUDDIES® TUSH TAGS

Version 1: The *Beanie Buddies* were introduced with a white tush tag with the "ty" logo in white letters inside a red heart. On the reverse, company and fabric information are printed in black ink.

Version 2: On the second *Buddies* tag, the words "The Beanie Buddies Collection®" are printed above the heart. The information on the back of the tag is now printed in red ink.

Version 3: The most recent tush tag looks like Version 2 except for the words "Shell 100% Tylon" on the front and "Inner Contents" on the back.

BEANIE KIDS™ SWING TAGS

The *Beanie Kids* swing tags are in the familiar red heart style with the "ty" logo in white. The heart is bordered in gold, and the name "Beanie Kids" is written in the upper-right corner in multi-colored, child-like letters. On the inside, "The Beanie Kids Collection™" and the countries of Ty Inc.'s corporate offices are listed on the left, while the right side lists the *Beanie Kids'* name with a trademark symbol. Beneath the name is the date of birth and a short poem. The official web site address for Ty Inc. appears on the bottom of the tag.

BEANIE KIDS™ TUSH TAGS

Ginger™

The tush tags of the *Beanie Kids* are similar to Version 8 *Beanie Babies* tush tags, except that they are looped. The tag is white with a hologram on the front. Inside the hologram are the words "Beanie Kids" and the "ty" heart logo. Stamped on the inside of the tush tag is an eight-digit alpha-numeric identification code. The back of the tag features a heart that disappears when touched.

TEENIE BEANIE BABIES™ SWING TAGS

1997 Version: These single-sheet tags feature a red, gold and white design on the front along with the puffy "ty" logo. The tag's reverse lists the name of the collection, the animal's name (both with the trademark symbols "TM/MC") and company information.

Teenie Beanie Babies™
Patti ™/MC ©Ty Inc.
Oakbrook, IL

Printed in China
Imprimé en Chine

1998 Version: The official Ty web site address is now printed on the back of the tag. The trademark symbols have been changed to read "TM/MC/MR," and a different font is used on all of the type. Small spacing differences can also be noted due to multiple production sources.

TM/MC/MR
Teenie Beanie Babies
Bongo TM/MC/MR ©Ty Inc.
Oakbrook, IL

www.ty.com
Printed in China
Imprimé en Chine

1999 Version: The 1999 tags are larger and fatter than their predecessors. The "ty" logo on the front is no longer gold-trimmed and a yellow star with the words "Original Teenie Beanie" has been added. The font on the reverse of the tag has been changed again, and the animal's type has been added after its name. symbol now reads only "TM."

Teenie Beanie Babies TM
Stretchy ©Ty Inc.
the Ostrich™ Oakbrook, IL

www.ty.com
Printed in China
Imprimé en Chine

TEENIE BEANIE BABIES™ TUSH TAGS

Teenie Beanie Babies tush tags feature the red "ty" heart logo, company and production information and the copyright date printed in red ink. The 1999 tush tags have a larger, fatter "ty" logo than before. The reverse sides of the tags are printed in black and contain content and manufacturing information. Small differences about the content information and the McDonald's corporate name appear on the 1999 tags.

© 1993 TY INC.,
OAKBROOK, IL
MADE IN CHINA

SIMON MARKETING, INC.
LOS ANGELES, CA.
ALL NEW MATERIALS
CONTENTS: HIGH DENSITY
POLYETHELENE PELLETS,
POLYESTER FIBERS
REG NO. PA-7674(HK)
MFD. FOR McDONALD'S®
MADE IN CHINA   RC

©1993 TY INC.,
OAKBROOK, IL
MADE IN CHINA

M-B SALES WESTMONT, IL.
ALL NEW MATERIALS
CONTENTS: HIGH DENSITY
POLYETHELENE PELLETS,
POLYESTER FIBERS
REG NO. PA5309HK
Mfd. for McDonald's
MADE IN CHINA   TS

How To Use Your Value Guide

Determining the market value of your collection is as easy as 1, 2, 3!

1. Record the price you paid and the tag generation for each piece in the "Price Paid" column. Use the key on the right to help identify the swing tag your *Beanie* has (see pages 36-41 for more tag information).

2. Find the value of each piece by looking at the dollar amount listed next to the corresponding swing tag heart in the "Market Value" column. For current pieces, write in the current market (retail) value. If a piece's value is not established, it is listed as "N/E." *Sports Promotion Beanie Babies* are marked in the Value Guide with the appropriate sports symbols (refer to the chart below). All current *Beanies* are rated as to how easy or difficult they are to find (see chart at bottom).

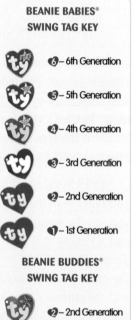

BEANIE BABIES® SWING TAG KEY

6 – 6th Generation

5 – 5th Generation

4 – 4th Generation

3 – 3rd Generation

2 – 2nd Generation

1 – 1st Generation

BEANIE BUDDIES® SWING TAG KEY

2 – 2nd Generation

1 – 1st Generation

SPORTS PROMOTION BEANIE BABIES® KEY

Canadian Special Olympics

Major League Baseball

National Basketball Association

National Football League

National Hockey League

Women's National Basketball Association

3. Add the "Price Paid" columns on each page and record the total in the "Page Totals" section at the bottom of each page. Do the same for the "Market Value." Copy your page totals onto pages 160-161 and add the sums together to get the "Grand Total" of your *Beanie* collection!

DEGREE OF DIFFICULTY RATINGS	
Just Released	*Hard To Find*
Easy To Find	*Very Hard To Find*
Moderate To Find	*Impossible To Find*

Beanie Kids™

The speculation is finally over! The January 2000 introduction of the *Beanie Kids* ended months of rumors and gossip surrounding the identity of Ty's mystery product. Consisting of five girls and four boys, this inaugural assortment of *Kids* are "Angel," "Boomer," "Chipper," "Curly," "Cutie," "Ginger," "Precious," "Rascal" and "Tumbles." Each one comes with a

poem and a birth date – just like their other *Beanie* friends. With cute faces, soft hair and adorable outfits, these *Beanie Kids* have become overnight celebrities in the world of Ty!

1

NEW!

Angel™
Kid · #0001
Issued: January 8, 2000
Current - Just Released

Birthdate: March 29, 1994
Be my best friend and then you will see,
how very, very special you are to me!

Price Paid

Market Value

❶ _____

2

NEW!

Boomer™
Kid · #0007
Issued: January 8, 2000
Current - Just Released

Birthdate: August 11, 1994
I like being noisy, it's lots of fun,
then I get attention from everyone!

Price Paid

Market Value

 ❶ _____

3

NEW!

Chipper™
Kid · #0008
Issued: January 8, 2000
Current - Just Released

Birthdate: July 20, 1997
Happy and cheerful, big hugs for all,
smiling and laughing - life is a ball!

Price Paid

Market Value

 ❶ _____

Page Totals	Price Paid	Market Value

COLLECTOR'S
VALUE GUIDE™

4

NEW!

Curly™
Kid · #0004
Issued: January 8, 2000
Current - Just Released

Birthdate: March 2, 1997
My curly hair is a sight to see,
a pretty bow makes me cute as can be!

Price Paid   Market Value
          ❶ _____

5

NEW!

Cutie™
Kid · #0005
Issued: January 8, 2000
Current - Just Released

Birthdate: December 26, 1996
I can't help but give you a hug,
in your arms is where I feel snug!

Price Paid   Market Value
          ❶ _____

6

NEW!

Ginger™
Kid · #0003
Issued: January 8, 2000
Current - Just Released

Birthdate: June 12, 1992
Everyone says I'm all sugar and spice,
so when we play, I'll always be nice!

Price Paid	Market Value
	❶ _____

7

NEW!

Precious™
Kid · #0002
Issued: January 8, 2000
Current - Just Released

Birthdate: May 15, 1993
Hey, look at me and give me a smile,
take me home and we'll play awhile!

Price Paid	Market Value
	❶ _____

Page Totals	Price Paid	Market Value

COLLECTOR'S
VALUE GUIDE™

8

NEW!

Rascal™

Kid · #0006
Issued: January 8, 2000
Current - Just Released

Birthdate: April 15, 1995
Hear me giggle and watch me dance,
I'll make you laugh, so give me a chance!

Price Paid   Market Value
❶ _____

9

NEW!

Tumbles™

Kid · #0009
Issued: January 8, 2000
Current - Just Released

Birthdate: September 3, 1996
A little bit naughty I'm known to be,
make sure you don't take your eyes off me!

Price Paid   Market Value
❶ _____

Beanie Babies®

When Ty Inc. announced that the company would retire all current *Beanies* on December 31, 1999, collectors were thrown into a panic. But the fate of the *Beanie Babies* was ultimately left in the hands of the fans, who responded with an overwhelming response to continue the production of *Beanie Babies*. The 20 new bean bag critters bring the total number of *Beanie Babies* to 240, and the *Beanie Babies* phenomenon seems well prepared for the new millennium.

#1 Bear™ (exclusive Ty sales representative gift)

Bear • N/A
Issued: December 12, 1998
Not Available In Retail Stores

Birthdate: N/A
Dedication Appearing On Special Tag
In appreciation of selling over several Billion dollars in 1998 and achieving the industry ranking of #1 in Gift sales, #1 in Collectible sales, #1 in Cash register area sales, #1 in Markup %, I present to you This Signed and Numbered bear!

Version	Dates Produced	Price Paid	Market Value
Original	Dec. 1998		Special Tag $9,200

1997 Teddy™

Bear • #4200
Issued: October 1, 1997
Retired: December 31, 1997

Birthdate: December 25, 1996
Beanie Babies are special no doubt
All filled with love – inside and out
Wishes for fun times filled with joy
Ty's holiday teddy is a magical toy!

Version	Dates Produced	Price Paid	Market Value
Original	Oct. 1997-Dec. 1997		④ $48

Page Totals	Price Paid	Market Value

COLLECTOR'S
VALUE GUIDE™

1998 Holiday Teddy™

Bear • #4204
Issued: September 30, 1998
Retired: December 31, 1998

Birthdate: December 25, 1998
Dressed in his PJ's, and ready for bed
Hugs given, good nights said
This little Beanie will stay close at night
Ready for a hug at first morning light!

3

Version	Issue Dates	Price Paid	Market Value
Original	Sept. 1998-Dec. 1998		🪙 $50

1999 Holiday Teddy™

Bear • #4257
Issued: August 31, 1999
Retired: December 23, 1999

Birthdate: December 25, 1999
Peace on Earth as the holidays grow near
The season is all about giving good cheer
With love and joy in your hearts
Lets all be friends as the century starts!

4

Version	Issue Dates	Price Paid	Market Value
Original	Aug. 1999-Dec. 1999		🪙 $35

1999 Signature Bear™

Bear • #4228
Issued: January 1, 1999
Retired: October 25, 1999

Birthdate: N/A
No Poem

5

Version	Issue Dates	Price Paid	Market Value
Original	Jan. 1999-Oct. 1999		🪙 $18

6

NEW!

2000 Signature Bear™

Bear · #4266
Issued: February 13, 2000
Current - Just Released

Birthdate: N/A
No Poem

Version	Issue Dates	Price Paid	Market Value
Original	Feb. 2000-Current		**6** $_____

7

Ally™

Alligator · #4032
Issued: June 25, 1994
Retired: October 1, 1997

Birthdate: March 14, 1994
When Ally gets out of classes
He wears a hat and dark glasses
He plays bass in a street band
He's the coolest gator in the land!

Version	Issue Dates	Price Paid	Market Value
Original	June 1994-Oct. 1997		**4** $45 **3** $120 **2** $260 **1** $425

8

Almond™

Bear · #4246
Issued: April 19, 1999
Retired: December 23, 1999

Birthdate: April 14, 1999
Leaving her den in early spring
So very hungry, she'll eat anything
Nuts, fruit, berries and fish
Mixed together make a great dish!

Version	Issue Dates	Price Paid	Market Value
Original	April 1999-Dec. 1999		**5** $10

Page Totals	Price Paid	Market Value

COLLECTOR'S
VALUE GUIDE™

Amber™

9

Cat • #4243
Issued: April 20, 1999
Retired: December 23, 1999

Birthdate: February 21, 1999
Sleeping all day and up all night
Waiting to pounce and give you a fright
She means no harm, just playing a game
She's very lovable and quite tame!

Version	Issue Dates	Price Paid	Market Value
Original	April 1999-Dec. 1999		⑤ $10

Ants™

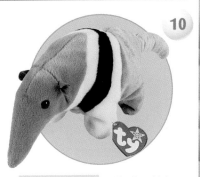

10

Anteater • #4195
Issued: May 30, 1998
Retired: December 31, 1998

Birthdate: November 7, 1997
Most anteaters love to eat bugs
But this little fellow gives big hugs
He'd rather dine on apple pie
Than eat an ant or harm a fly!

Version	Issue Dates	Price Paid	Market Value
Original	May 1998-Dec. 1998		⑤ $10

Aurora™

11

NEW!

Polar Bear • #4271
Issued: February 13, 2000
Current - Just Released

Birthdate: February 3, 2000
The midnight sun puts on a show
For all the polar bears below
Under ribbons of shining light
Aurora hugs you and says goodnight!

Version	Issue Dates	Price Paid	Market Value
Original	Feb. 2000-Current		⑥ $_____

COLLECTOR'S
VALUE GUIDE™

	Price Paid	Market Value
Page Totals		

12

B.B. Bear™

Bear • #4253
Issued: Summer 1999
Retired: December 23, 1999

Birthdate: N/A
This birthday Beanie was made for you
Hope your wishes and dreams come true
Be happy today and tomorrow too
Let's all celebrate the whole year through!

Version	Issue Dates	Price Paid	Market Value
Original	Summer 1999-Dec. 1999		$25

13

Baldy™

Eagle • #4074
Issued: May 11, 1997
Retired: May 1, 1998

Birthdate: February 17, 1996
Hair on his head is quite scant
We suggest Baldy get a transplant
Watching over the land of the free
Hair in his eyes would make it hard to see!

Version	Issue Dates	Price Paid	Market Value
Original	May 1997-May 1998		🌀 $16 🌀 $20

14

A   B

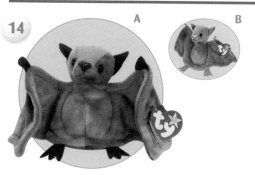

Batty™

Bat • #4035
Issued: October 1, 1997
Retired: March 31, 1999

Birthdate: October 29, 1996
Bats may make some people jitter
Please don't be scared of this critter
If you're lonely or have nothing to do
This Beanie Baby would love to hug you!

Version	Issue Dates	Price Paid	Market Value
A. Tie-dye	Jan. 1999-March 1999		🌀 $18
B. Brown	Est Oct. 1997-Jan. 1999		🌀 $11 🌀 $12

Page Totals	Price Paid	Market Value

COLLECTOR'S
VALUE GUIDE™

Beak™

Kiwi • #4211
Issued: September 30, 1998
Retired: December 23, 1999

15

Birthdate: February 3, 1998
Isn't this just the funniest bird?
When we saw her, we said "how absurd"
Looks aren't everything, this we know
Her love for you, she's sure to show!

Version	Issue Dates	Price Paid	Market Value
Original	Sept. 1998-Dec. 1999		⑤ $8

Bernie™

St. Bernard • #4109
Issued: January 1, 1997
Retired: September 22, 1998

16

Birthdate: October 3, 1996
This little dog can't wait to grow
To rescue people lost in the snow
Don't let him out – keep him on your shelf
He doesn't know how to rescue himself!

Version	Issue Dates	Price Paid	Market Value
Original	Jan. 1997-Sept. 1998		⑤ $12 ④ $14

Bessie™

Cow • #4009
Issued: June 3, 1995
Retired: October 1, 1997

17

Birthdate: June 27, 1995
Bessie the cow likes to dance and sing
Because music is her favorite thing
Every night when you are counting sheep
She'll sing you a song to help you sleep!

Version	Issue Dates	Price Paid	Market Value
Original	June 1995-Oct. 1997		④ $57 ③ $115

	Price Paid	Market Value
Page Totals		

18

Billionaire bear™

(exclusive Ty employee gift)

Bear • N/A
Issued: September 26, 1998
Not Available In Retail Stores

Birthdate: N/A
Dedication Appearing On Special Tag
In recognition of value and
contributions in shipping over
a billion dollars since Jan '98,
I present to you this exclusive signed bear!

Version	Issue Dates	Price Paid	Market Value
Original	Sept. 1998		Special Tag $2,750

19

Billionaire 2™

(exclusive Ty employee gift)

Bear • N/A
Issued: September 12, 1999
Not Available In Retail Stores

Birthdate: N/A
Dedication Appearing On Special Tag
Ty is the company that can't be beat
Mattel and Hasbro can take a back seat
We did it again and it was fun
In the toy biz, we're #1!

Version	Issue Dates	Price Paid	Market Value
Original	Sept. 1999		Special Tag $5,800

20

Blackie™

Bear • #4011
Issued: June 25, 1994
Retired: September 15, 1998

Birthdate: July 15, 1994
Living in a national park
He only played after dark
Then he met his friend Cubbie
Now they play when it's sunny!

Version	Issue Dates	Price Paid	Market Value
Original	June 1994-Sept. 1998		⑤ $15 ④ $15
			③ $82 ② $230
			① $350

Page Totals	Price Paid	Market Value

COLLECTOR'S
VALUE GUIDE™

Blizzard™

21

Tiger · #4163
Issued: May 11, 1997
Retired: May 1, 1998

Birthdate: December 12, 1996
In the mountains, where it's snowy and cold
Lives a beautiful tiger, I've been told
Black and white, she's hard to compare
Of all the tigers, she is most rare!

Version	Issue Dates	Price Paid	Market Value
Original	May 1997-May 1998		⑤ $16 ④ $17

Bones™

22

Dog · #4001
Issued: June 25, 1994
Retired: May 1, 1998

Birthdate: January 18, 1994
Bones is a dog that loves to chew
Chairs and tables and a smelly old shoe
"You're so destructive" all would shout
But that all stopped, when his teeth
Fell out!

Version	Issue Dates	Price Paid	Market Value
Original	June 1994-May 1998		⑤ $17 ④ $18
			③ $95 ② $230
			① $400

Bongo™

23

(name changed from "Nana™")

Monkey · #4067
Issued: June 3, 1995
Retired: December 31, 1998

Birthdate: August 17, 1995
Bongo the monkey lives in a tree
The happiest monkey you'll ever see
In his spare time he plays the guitar
One of these days he will be a big star!

B   A

Version	Issue Dates	Price Paid	Market Value
A. Tan Tail	June 1995-Dec. 1998		⑤ $12 ④ $13
			③ $130
B. Brown Tail	Feb. 1996-June 1996		④ $55 ③ $165

Page Totals	Price Paid	Market Value

24

Britannia™
(exclusive to the United Kingdom)

Bear · #4601
Issued: December 31, 1997
Retired: July 26, 1999

Birthdate: December 15, 1997
Britannia the bear will sail the sea
So she can be with you and me
She's always sure to catch the tide
And wear the Union Flag with pride

Version	Issue Dates	Price Paid	Market Value
Original	Dec. 1997-July 1999		💲5 $125

25

Bronty™

Brontosaurus · #4085
Issued: June 3, 1995
Retired: June 15, 1996

Birthdate: N/A
No Poem

Version	Issue Dates	Price Paid	Market Value
Original	June 1995-June 1996		💲3 $750

26

Brownie™
(name changed to "Cubbie™")

Bear · #4010
Issued: January 8, 1994
Retired: 1994

Birthdate: N/A
No Poem

Version	Issue Dates	Price Paid	Market Value
Original	Jan. 1994-1994		💲1 $3,200

Page Totals	Price Paid	Market Value

COLLECTOR'S
VALUE GUIDE™

Bruno™

Dog · #4183
Issued: December 31, 1997
Retired: September 18, 1998

27

Birthdate: September 9, 1997
Bruno the dog thinks he's a brute
But all the other Beanies think he's cute
He growls at his tail and runs in a ring
And everyone says, "Oh, how darling!"

Version	Issue Dates	Price Paid	Market Value
Original	Dec. 1997-Sept. 1998		⑤ $9

Bubbles™

Fish · #4078
Issued: June 3, 1995
Retired: May 11, 1997

28

Birthdate: July 2, 1995
All day long Bubbles likes to swim
She never gets tired of flapping her fins
Bubbles lived in a sea of blue
Now she is ready to come home with you!

Version	Issue Dates	Price Paid	Market Value
Original	June 1995-May 1997		④ $125 ③ $190

Bucky™

Beaver · #4016
Issued: January 7, 1996
Retired: December 31, 1997

29

Birthdate: June 8, 1995
Bucky's teeth are as shiny as can be
Often used for cutting trees
He hides in his dam night and day
Maybe for you he will come out and play!

Version	Issue Dates	Price Paid	Market Value
Original	Jan. 1996-Dec. 1997		④ $32 ③ $90

30

Bumble™
Bee • #4045
Issued: June 3, 1995
Retired: June 15, 1996

Birthdate: October 16, 1995
Bumble the bee will not sting you
It is only love that this bee will bring you
So don't be afraid to give this bee a hug
Because Bumble the bee is a love-bug.

Version	Issue Dates	Price Paid	Market Value
Original	June 1995-June 1996		❹ $485 ❸ $450

31

NEW!

Bushy™
Lion • #4285
Issued: February 13, 2000
Current - Just Released

Birthdate: January 27, 2000
I won't roar – I'll purr instead
So always pat me on the head
A cuddly kitten I promise to be
If you'll come over and play with me!

Version	Issue Dates	Price Paid	Market Value
Original	Feb. 2000-Current		❻ $_____

32

Butch™
Bull Terrier • #4227
Issued: January 1, 1999
Retired: December 23, 1999

Birthdate: October 2, 1998
Going to the pet shop to buy dog food
I ran into Butch in a good mood
"Come to the pet shop down the street"
"Be a good dog, I'll buy you a treat!"

Version	Issue Dates	Price Paid	Market Value
Original	Jan. 1999-Dec. 1999		❺ $9

Page Totals	Price Paid	Market Value

COLLECTOR'S
VALUE GUIDE™

Canyon™
Cougar • #4212
Issued: September 30, 1998
Retired: August 16, 1999

Birthdate: May 29, 1998
I climb rocks and really run fast
Try to catch me, it's a blast
Through the mountains, I used to roam
Now in your room, I'll call it home!

33

Version	Issue Dates	Price Paid	Market Value
Original	Sept. 1998-Aug. 1999		💰 $9

Caw™
Crow • #4071
Issued: June 3, 1995
Retired: June 15, 1996

Birthdate: N/A
No Poem

34

Version	Issue Dates	Price Paid	Market Value
Original	June 1995-June 1996		💰 $550

Cheeks™
Baboon • #4250
Issued: April 17, 1999
Retired: December 23, 1999

Birthdate: May 18, 1999
Don't confuse me with an ape
I have a most unusual shape
My cheeks are round and ty-dyed red
On my behind as well as my head!

35

Version	Issue Dates	Price Paid	Market Value
Original	April 1999-Dec. 1999		💰 $11

	Price Paid	Market Value
Page Totals		

36

Chilly™
Polar Bear • #4012
Issued: June 25, 1994
Retired: January 7, 1996

Birthdate: N/A
No Poem

Version	Issue Dates	Price Paid	Market Value
Original	June 1994-Jan. 1996		③ $1,500
			② $1,700
			① $2,000

37

Chip™
Cat • #4121
Issued: May 11, 1997
Retired: March 31, 1999

Birthdate: January 26, 1996
Black and gold, brown and white
The shades of her coat are quite a sight
At mixing her colors she was a master
On anyone else it would be a disaster!

Version	Issue Dates	Price Paid	Market Value
Original	May 1997-March 1999		⑤ $10 ④ $10

38

Chipper™
Chipmunk • #4259
Issued: August 31, 1999
Retired: December 23, 1999

Birthdate: April 21, 1999
I'm quick, I'm fast, I don't make a peep
But I love to snuggle when I sleep
Take me along when you go play
And I'll make sure you have a nice day!

Version	Issue Dates	Price Paid	Market Value
Original	Aug. 1999-Dec. 1999		⑤ $11

Page Totals	Price Paid	Market Value

COLLECTOR'S
VALUE GUIDE™

Chocolate™

Moose · #4015
Issued: January 8, 1994
Retired: December 31, 1998

Birthdate: April 27, 1993
Licorice, gum and peppermint candy
This moose always has these handy
There is one more thing he likes to eat
Can you guess his favorite sweet?

39

Version	Issue Dates	Price Paid	Market Value
Original	Jan. 1994-Dec. 1998		⑤ $10 ④ $10
			❸ $90 ❷ $280
			❶ $520

Chops™

Lamb · #4019
Issued: January 7, 1996
Retired: January 1, 1997

Birthdate: May 3, 1996
Chops is a little lamb
This lamb you'll surely know
Because every path that you may take
This lamb is sure to go!

40

Version	Issue Dates	Price Paid	Market Value
Original	Jan. 1996-Jan. 1997		④ $130 ❸ $200

Claude™

Crab · #4083
Issued: May 11, 1997
Retired: December 31, 1998

Birthdate: September 3, 1996
Claude the crab paints by the sea
A famous artist he hopes to be
But the tide came in and his paints fell
Now his art is on his shell!

41

Version	Issue Dates	Price Paid	Market Value
Original	May 1997-Dec. 1998		⑤ $11 ④ $13

42

Clubby® (Beanie Babies® Official Club™ members' exclusive)

Bear • N/A
Issued: May 1, 1998
Retired: March 15, 1999

Birthdate: July 7, 1998
Wearing his club pin for all to see
He's a proud member like you and me
Made especially with you in mind
Clubby the bear is one of a kind!

Version	Issue Dates	Price Paid	Market Value
Original	May 1998-March 1999		$42

43

Clubby II™ (Beanie Babies® Official Club™ members' exclusive)

Bear • N/A
Issued: March 31, 1999
Current: Hard To Find

Birthdate: March 9, 1999
A proud club member, named Clubby II
My color is special, a purplish hue
Take me along to your favorite place
Carry me in my platinum case!

Version	Issue Dates	Price Paid	Market Value
Original	March 1999-Dec. 1999		$30

44

Congo™

Gorilla • #4160
Issued: June 15, 1996
Retired: December 31, 1998

Birthdate: November 9, 1996
Black as the night and fierce is he
On the ground or in a tree
Strong and mighty as the Congo
He's related to our Bongo!

Version	Issue Dates	Price Paid	Market Value
Original	June 1996-Dec. 1998		$11 $12

Page Totals	Price Paid	Market Value

COLLECTOR'S
VALUE GUIDE™

Coral™

Fish · #4079
Issued: June 3, 1995
Retired: January 1, 1997

Birthdate: March 2, 1995
Coral is beautiful, as you know
Made of colors in the rainbow
Whether it's pink, yellow or blue
These colors were chosen just for you!

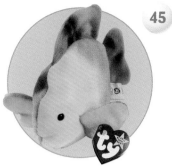

45

Version	Issue Dates	Price Paid	Market Value
Original	June 1995-Jan. 1997		④ $150 ③ $215

Crunch™

Shark · #4130
Issued: January 1, 1997
Retired: September 24, 1998

Birthdate: January 13, 1996
What's for breakfast? What's for lunch?
Yum! Delicious! Munch, munch, munch!
He's eating everything by the bunch
That's the reason we named him Crunch!

46

Version	Issue Dates	Price Paid	Market Value
Original	Jan. 1997-Sept. 1998		⑤ $11 ④ $12

Cubbie™ (name changed from "Brownie™")

Bear · #4010
Issued: January 8, 1994
Retired: December 31, 1997

Birthdate: November 14, 1993
Cubbie used to eat crackers and honey
And what happened to him was funny
He was stung by fourteen bees
Now Cubbie eats broccoli and cheese!

47

Version	Issue Dates	Price Paid	Market Value
Original	Jan. 1994-Dec. 1997		⑤ $22 ④ $30
			③ $150 ② $290
			① $550

Page Totals	Price Paid	Market Value

48

Curly™

Bear · #4052
Issued: June 15, 1996
Retired: December 31, 1998

Birthdate: April 12, 1996
A bear so cute with hair that's Curly
You will love and want him surely
To this bear always be true
He will be a friend to you!

Version	Issue Dates	Price Paid	Market Value
Original	June 1996-Dec. 1998		⑤ $20　④ $22

49

Daisy™

Cow · #4006
Issued: June 25, 1994
Retired: September 15, 1998

Birthdate: May 10, 1994
Daisy drinks milk each night
So her coat is shiny and bright
Milk is good for your hair and skin
What a way for your day to begin!

Version	Issue Dates	Price Paid	Market Value
Original	June 1994-Sept. 1998		⑤ $13　④ $15
			③ $110　② $250
			① $370

50

A　B
C
D

Derby™

Horse · #4008
Issued: June 3, 1995
Retired: May 26, 1999

Birthdate: September 16, 1995
All the other horses used to tattle
Because Derby never wore his saddle
He left the stables, and the horses too
Just so Derby can be with you!

Version	Issue Dates	Price Paid	Market Value
A. Star/Fluffy Mane	Jan. 1999-May 1999		⑤ $12
B. Star/Coarse Mane	Dec. 1997-Dec. 1998		⑤ $13
C. No Star/Coarse Mane	Est. Late 1995-Dec. 1997		④ $20　③ $360
D. No Star/Fine Mane	Est. June 1995-Est. Late 1995		③ $2,250

	Price Paid	Market Value
Page Totals		

Digger™

Crab · #4027
Issued: June 25, 1994
Retired: May 11, 1997

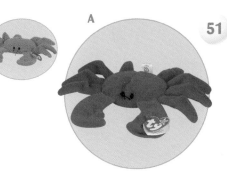

51

Birthdate: August 23, 1995
Digging in the sand and walking sideways
That's how Digger spends her days
Hard on the outside but sweet deep inside
Basking in the sun and riding the tide!

Version	Issue Dates	Price Paid	Market Value
A. Red	June 1995-May 1997		**4** $90 **3** $175
B. Orange	June 1994-June 1995		**3** $575 **2** $700
			1 $850

Doby™

Doberman · #4110
Issued: January 1, 1997
Retired: December 31, 1998

52

Birthdate: October 9, 1996
This dog is little but he has might
Keep him close when you sleep at night
He lays around with nothing to do
Until he sees it's time to protect you!

Version	Issue Dates	Price Paid	Market Value
Original	Jan. 1997-Dec. 1998		**5** $11 **4** $12

Doodle™

(name changed to "Strut™")

Rooster · #4171
Issued: May 11, 1997
Retired: 1997

53

Birthdate: March 8, 1996
Listen closely to "cock-a-doodle-doo"
What's the rooster saying to you?
Hurry, wake up sleepy head
We have lots to do, get out of bed!

Version	Issue Dates	Price Paid	Market Value
Original	May 1997-1997		**4** $32

54

Dotty™
Dalmatian • #4100
Issued: May 11, 1997
Retired: December 31, 1998

Birthdate: October 17, 1996
The Beanies all thought it was a big joke
While writing her tag, their ink pen broke
She got in the way, and got all spotty
So now the Beanies call her Dotty!

Version	Issue Dates	Price Paid	Market Value
Original	May 1997-Dec. 1998		❺ $12 ❹ $13

55

Early™
Robin • #4190
Issued: May 30, 1998
Retired: December 23, 1999

Birthdate: March 20, 1997
Early is a red breasted robin
For a worm he'll soon be bobbin'
Always known as a sign of spring
This happy robin loves to sing!

Version	Issue Dates	Price Paid	Market Value
Original	May 1998-Dec. 1999		❺ $8

56

Ears™
Rabbit • #4018
Issued: January 7, 1996
Retired: May 1, 1998

Birthdate: April 18, 1995
He's been eating carrots so long
Didn't understand what was wrong
Couldn't see the board during classes
Until the doctor gave him glasses!

Version	Issue Dates	Price Paid	Market Value
Original	Jan. 1996-May 1998		❺ $13 ❹ $14
			❸ $75

	Price Paid	Market Value
Page Totals		

COLLECTOR'S
VALUE GUIDE™

Echo™

57

Dolphin • #4180
Issued: May 11, 1997
Retired: May 1, 1998

Birthdate: December 21, 1996
Echo the dolphin lives in the sea
Playing with her friends, like you and me
Through the waves she echoes the sound
"I'm so glad to have you around!"

Version	Issue Dates	Price Paid	Market Value
Original	May 1997-May 1998		5 $15 4 $17

Eggbert™

58

Chick • #4232
Issued: January 1, 1999
Retired: July 28, 1999

Birthdate: April 10, 1998
Cracking her shell taking a peek
Look, she's playing hide and seek
Ready or not, here I come
Take me home and have some fun!

Version	Issue Dates	Price Paid	Market Value
Original	Jan. 1999-July 1999		5 $13

Erin™

59

Bear • #4186
Issued: January 31, 1998
Retired: May 21, 1999

Birthdate: March 17, 1997
Named after the beautiful Emerald Isle
This Beanie Baby will make you smile,
A bit of luck, a pot of gold,
Light up the faces, both young and old!

Version	Issue Dates	Price Paid	Market Value
Original	Jan. 1998-May 1999		5 $20

Page Totals	Price Paid	Market Value

60

Eucalyptus™
Koala • #4240
Issued: April 8, 1999
Retired: October 27, 1999

Birthdate: April 28, 1999
Koalas climb with grace and ease
To the top branches of the trees
Sleeping by day under a gentle breeze
Feeding at night on two pounds of leaves!

Version	Issue Dates	Price Paid	Market Value
Original	Apr. 1999-Oct. 1999		💲 $14

61

Ewey™
Lamb • #4219
Issued: January 1, 1999
Retired: July 19, 1999

Birthdate: March 1, 1998
Needles and yarn, Ewey loves to knit
Making sweaters with perfect fit
Happy to make one for you and me
Showing off hers, for all to see!

Version	Issue Dates	Price Paid	Market Value
Original	Jan. 1999-July 1999		💲 $12

62

Fetch™
Golden Retriever • #4189
Issued: May 30, 1998
Retired: December 31, 1998

Birthdate: February 4, 1997
Fetch is alert at the crack of dawn
Walking through dew drops on the lawn
Always golden, loyal and true
This little puppy is the one for you!

Version	Issue Dates	Price Paid	Market Value
Original	May 1998-Dec. 1998		💲 $14

Page Totals	Price Paid	Market Value

COLLECTOR'S
VALUE GUIDE™

Flash™

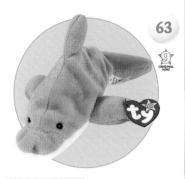

Dolphin · #4021
Issued: January 8, 1994
Retired: May 11, 1997

Birthdate: May 13, 1993
You know dolphins are a smart breed
Our friend Flash knows how to read
Splash the whale is the one who taught her
Although reading is difficult under the water!

Version	Issue Dates	Price Paid	Market Value
Original	Jan. 1994-May 1997		❹ $100 ❸ $165 ❷ $330 ❶ $500

Fleece™

Lamb · #4125
Issued: January 1, 1997
Retired: December 31, 1998

Birthdate: March 21, 1996
Fleece would like to sing a lullaby
But please be patient, she's rather shy
When you sleep, keep her by your ear
Her song will leave you nothing to fear.

Version	Issue Dates	Price Paid	Market Value
Original	Jan. 1997-Dec. 1998		❺ $12 ❹ $13

Fleecie™

NEW!

Lamb · #4279
Issued: February 13, 2000
Current - Just Released

Birthdate: January 26, 2000
Fleecie is cuddly and soft as can be
Give her a hug and then you will see
When you hold her close to your ear
You'll hear her whisper "I love you, dear!"

Version	Issue Dates	Price Paid	Market Value
Original	Feb. 2000-Current		❻ $_____

66

Flip™
Cat • #4012
Issued: January 7, 1996
Retired: October 1, 1997

Birthdate: February 28, 1995
Flip the cat is an acrobat
She loves playing on her mat
This cat flips with such grace and flair
She can somersault in mid air!

Version	Issue Dates	Price Paid	Market Value
Original	Jan. 1996-Oct. 1997		④ $32 ❸ $90

67

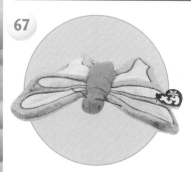

Flitter™
Butterfly • #4255
Issued: Summer 1999
Retired: December 23, 1999

Birthdate: June 2, 1999
I did not know what I was to be
Covered in fuzz, it was hard to see
Now a butterfly, what a beautiful sight
On silken wings I take to flight!

Version	Issue Dates	Price Paid	Market Value
Original	Summer 1999-Dec. 1999		❺ $20

68

Floppity™
Bunny • #4118
Issued: January 1, 1997
Retired: May 1, 1998

Birthdate: May 28, 1996
Floppity hops from here to there
Searching for eggs without a care
Lavender coat from head to toe
All dressed up and nowhere to go!

Version	Issue Dates	Price Paid	Market Value
Original	Jan. 1997-May 1998		❺ $17 ④ $18

Page Totals	Price Paid	Market Value

COLLECTOR'S
VALUE GUIDE™

Flutter™

Butterfly • #4043
Issued: June 3, 1995
Retired: June 15, 1996

69

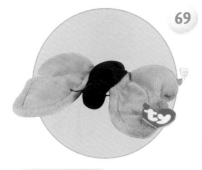

Birthdate: N/A
No Poem

Version	Issue Dates	Price Paid	Market Value
Original	June 1995-June 1996		❸ $800

Fortune™

Panda • #4196
Issued: May 30, 1998
Retired: August 24, 1999

70

Birthdate: December 6, 1997
Nibbling on a bamboo tree
This little panda is hard to see
You're so lucky with this one you found
Only a few are still around!

Version	Issue Dates	Price Paid	Market Value
Original	May 1998-Aug. 1999		❺ $12

Freckles™

Leopard • #4066
Issued: June 15, 1996
Retired: December 31, 1998

71

Birthdate: June 3, 1996
or July 28, 1996
From the trees he hunts prey
In the night and in the day
He's the king of camouflage
Look real close, he's no mirage!

Version	Issue Dates	Price Paid	Market Value
Original	June 1996-Dec. 1998		❺ $12 ❹ $13

72

NEW!

Frigid™
Penguin · #4270
Issued: February 13, 2000
Current - Just Released

Birthdate: January 23, 2000
Waddling on the slippery ice
Frigid thinks the cold is nice
He jumps into the water below
Then does it again, he loves it so!

Version	Issue Dates	Price Paid	Market Value
Original	Feb. 2000-Current		⑥ $_____

73

Fuzz™
Bear · #4237
Issued: January 1, 1999
Retired: December 23, 1999

Birthdate: July 23, 1998
Look closely at this handsome bear
His texture is really quite rare.
With golden highlights in his hair
He has class, style and flair!

Version	Issue Dates	Price Paid	Market Value
Original	Jan. 1999-Dec. 1999		⑤ $16

74

Garcia™
Bear · #4051
Issued: January 7, 1996
Retired: May 11, 1997

Birthdate: August 1, 1995
The Beanies use to follow him around
Because Garcia traveled from town to town
He's pretty popular as you can see
Some even say he's legendary!

Version	Issue Dates	Price Paid	Market Value
Original	Jan. 1996-May 1997		④ $165 ③ $250

Page Totals	Price Paid	Market Value

COLLECTOR'S
VALUE GUIDE™

Germania™
(exclusive to Germany)

Bear • #4236
Issued: January 1, 1999
Retired: December 23, 1999

75

Geburtstag: Oktober 3, 1990
Einigkeit und Recht und Freiheit
ist der Deutschen Einheistlied.
Allen Kindern brav und fein
soll dieser Bär das Liebste sein.

Poem Translation
Unity and Justice and Freedom
Is the song of German unity.
All good little girls and boys
Should love this little German bear.

Version	Issue Dates	Price Paid	Market Value (in U.S. market)
Original	Jan. 1999-Dec. 1999		🌀 $190

GiGi™

Poodle • #4191
Issued: May 30, 1998
Retired: December 23, 1999

76

Birthdate: April 7, 1997
Prancing and dancing all down the street
Thinking her hairdo is oh so neat
Always so careful in the wind and rain
She's a dog that is anything but plain!

Version	Issue Dates	Price Paid	Market Value
Original	May 1998-Dec. 1999		🌀 $8

Glory™

Bear • #4188
Issued: May 30, 1998
Retired: December 31, 1998

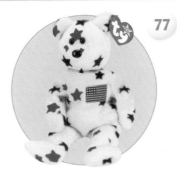

77

Birthdate: July 4, 1997
Wearing the flag for all to see
Symbol of freedom for you and me
Red white and blue – Independence Day
Happy Birthday USA!

Version	Issue Dates	Price Paid	Market Value
Original	May 1998-Dec. 1998		🌀 $36

78

NEW!

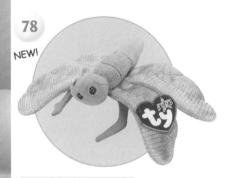

Glow™
Lightning Bug · #4283
Issued: February 13, 2000
Current - Just Released

Birthdate: January 4, 2000
To find me when you want to play
Look for my light to guide the way
I'll be the brightest in the park
I'm the Beanie that glows in the dark!

Version	Issue Dates	Price Paid	Market Value
Original	Feb. 2000-Current		🪙 $_____

79

Goatee™
Mountain Goat · #4235
Issued: January 1, 1999
Retired: December 23, 1999

Birthdate: November 4, 1998
Though she's hungry, she's in a good mood
Searching through garbage, tin cans for food
For Goatee the goat, it's not a big deal
Anything at all makes a fine meal!

Version	Issue Dates	Price Paid	Market Value
Original	Jan. 1999-Dec. 1999		🪙 $9

80

Gobbles™
Turkey · #4034
Issued: October 1, 1997
Retired: March 31, 1999

Birthdate: November 27, 1996
Gobbles the turkey loves to eat
Once a year she has a feast
I have a secret I'd like to divulge
If she eats too much her tummy will bulge!

Version	Issue Dates	Price Paid	Market Value	
Original	Oct. 1997-March 1999		🪙 $10	🪙 $12

Page Totals	Price Paid	Market Value

COLLECTOR'S
VALUE GUIDE™

Goldie™

Goldfish • #4023
Issued: June 25, 1994
Retired: December 31, 1997

81

Birthdate: November 14, 1994
She's got rhythm, she's got soul
What more to like in a fish bowl?
Through sound waves Goldie swam
Because this goldfish likes to jam!

Version	Issue Dates	Price Paid	Market Value
Original	June 1994-Dec. 1997		⑤ $38 ④ $38
			③ $105 ② $260
			① $430

Goochy™

Jellyfish • #4230
Issued: January 1, 1999
Retired: December 23, 1999

82

Birthdate: November 18, 1998
Swirl, swish, squirm and wiggle
Listen closely, hear him giggle
The most ticklish jellyfish you'll ever meet
Even though he has no feet!

Version	Issue Dates	Price Paid	Market Value
Original	Jan. 1999-Dec. 1999		⑤ $10

Grace™

Bunny • #4274
Issued: February 13, 2000
Current - Just Released

83

NEW!

Birthdate: February 10, 2000
Please watch over me night and day
When I sleep and when I pray
Keep me safe from up above
With special blessings of your love!

Version	Issue Dates	Price Paid	Market Value
Original	Feb. 2000-Current		⑥ $_____

84

Gracie™

Swan • #4126
Issued: January 1, 1997
Retired: May 1, 1998

Birthdate: June 17, 1996
As a duckling, she was confused,
Birds on the lake were quite amused.
Poking fun until she would cry,
Now the most beautiful swan at Ty!

Version	Issue Dates	Price Paid	Market Value
Original	Jan. 1997-May 1998		⑤ $14 ④ $15

85

Groovy™

Bear • #4256
Issued: August 31, 1999
Retired: December 23, 1999

Birthdate: January 10, 1999
Wearing colors of the rainbow
Making good friends wherever I go
Take me with you, don't let me stay
I need your love all night and day!

Version	Issue Dates	Price Paid	Market Value
Original	Aug. 1999-Dec. 1999		⑤ $27

86

Grunt™

Razorback • #4092
Issued: January 7, 1996
Retired: May 11, 1997

Birthdate: July 19, 1995
Some Beanies think Grunt is tough
No surprise, he's scary enough
But if you take him home you'll see
Grunt is the sweetest Beanie Baby!

Version	Issue Dates	Price Paid	Market Value
Original	Jan. 1996-May 1997		④ $130 ③ $185

Page Totals	Price Paid	Market Value

COLLECTOR'S
VALUE GUIDE™

Halo™

Angel Bear • #4208
Issued: September 30, 1998
Retired: November 19, 1999

Birthdate: August 31, 1998
When you sleep, I'm always here
Don't be afraid, I am near
Watching over you with lots of love
Your guardian angel from up above!

Version	Issue Dates	Price Paid	Market Value
Original	Sept. 1998-Nov. 1999		⑤ $16

Halo II™

Angel Bear • #4269
Issued: February 13, 2000
Current - Just Released

NEW!

Birthdate: January 14, 2000
Little angel up above
Guard me with your special love
Make sure that you will always be
By my side and close to me!

Version	Issue Dates	Price Paid	Market Value
Original	Feb. 2000-Current		⑥ $_____

Happy™

Hippo • #4061
Issued: June 25, 1994
Retired: May 1, 1998

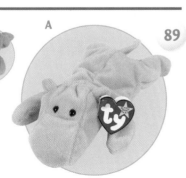

B   A

Birthdate: February 25, 1994
Happy the Hippo loves to wade
In the river and in the shade
When Happy shoots water out of his snout
You know he's happy without a doubt!

Version	Issue Dates	Price Paid	Market Value
A. Lavender	June 1995-May 1998		⑤ $22 ④ $24 ③ $180
B. Gray	June 1994-June 1995		③ $520 ② $620 ① $785

Page Totals	Price Paid	Market Value

90

Hippie™
Bunny · #4218
Issued: January 1, 1999
Retired: July 12, 1999

Birthdate: May 4, 1998
Hippie fell into the dye, they say
While coloring eggs, one spring day
From the tips of his ears, down to his toes
Colors of springtime, he proudly shows!

Version	Issue Dates	Price Paid	Market Value
Original	Jan. 1999-July 1999		⑤ $22

91

Hippity™
Bunny · #4119
Issued: January 1, 1997
Retired: May 1, 1998

Birthdate: June 1, 1996
Hippity is a cute little bunny
Dressed in green, he looks quite funny
Twitching his nose in the air
Sniffing a flower here and there!

Version	Issue Dates	Price Paid	Market Value
Original	Jan. 1997-May 1998		⑤ $20 ④ $22

92

Hissy™
Snake · #4185
Issued: December 31, 1997
Retired: March 31, 1999

Birthdate: April 4, 1997
Curled and coiled and ready to play
He waits for you patiently every day
He'll keep his best friend, but not his skin
And stay with you through thick and thin.

Version	Issue Dates	Price Paid	Market Value
Original	Dec. 1997-Mar. 1999		⑤ $9

Page Totals	Price Paid	Market Value

COLLECTOR'S
VALUE GUIDE™

Honks™

93

Goose • #4258
Issued: August 31, 1999
Retired: December 23, 1999

Birthdate: March 11, 1999
Honks the goose likes to fly away
South for Winter he will stay
When Spring comes back, North he will fly
And swim in ponds and lakes nearby!

Version	Issue Dates	Price Paid	Market Value
Original	Aug. 1999-Dec. 1999		⑤ $10

Hoot™

94

Owl • #4073
Issued: January 7, 1996
Retired: October 1, 1997

Birthdate: August 9, 1995
Late to bed, late to rise
Nevertheless, Hoot's quite wise
Studies by candlelight, nothing new
Like a president, do you know Whooo?

Version	Issue Dates	Price Paid	Market Value	
Original	Jan. 1996-Oct. 1997		④ $38	③ $105

Hope™

95

Bear • #4213
Issued: January 1, 1999
Retired: December 23, 1999

Birthdate: March 23, 1998
Every night when it's time for bed
Fold your hands and bow your head
An angelic face, a heart that's true
You have a friend to pray with you!

Version	Issue Dates	Price Paid	Market Value
Original	Jan. 1999-Dec. 1999		⑤ $14

COLLECTOR'S
VALUE GUIDE™

Page Totals	Price Paid	Market Value

96

Hoppity™
Bunny · #4117
Issued: January 1, 1997
Retired: May 1, 1998

Birthdate: April 3, 1996
Hopscotch is what she likes to play
If you don't join in, she'll hop away
So play a game if you have the time,
She likes to play, rain or shine!

Version	Issue Dates	Price Paid	Market Value
Original	Jan. 1997-May 1998		⑤ $17 ④ $18

97

Humphrey™
Camel · #4060
Issued: June 25, 1994
Retired: June 15, 1995

Birthdate: N/A
No Poem

Version	Issue Dates	Price Paid	Market Value
Original	June 1994-June 1995		③ $1,850 ② $2,050 ① $2,450

98

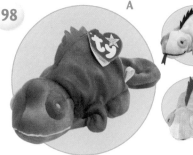

A   B   C

Iggy™
Iguana · #4038
Issued: December 31, 1997
Retired: March 31, 1999

Birthdate: August 12, 1997
Sitting on a rock, basking in the sun
Is this iguana's idea of fun
Towel and glasses, book and beach chair
His life is so perfect without a care!

Version	Issue Dates	Price Paid	Market Value
A. Blue/No Tongue	Mid 1998-Mar. 1999		⑤ $11
B. Tie-dye/With Tongue	June 1998-Mid 1998		⑤ $11
C. Tie-dye/No Tongue	Dec. 1997-June 1998		⑤ $11

Page Totals	Price Paid	Market Value

COLLECTOR'S
VALUE GUIDE™

Inch™

Inchworm · #4044
Issued: June 3, 1995
Retired: May 1, 1998

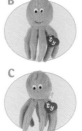

99

Birthdate: September 3, 1995
Inch the worm is a friend of mine
He goes so slow all the time
Inching around from here to there
Traveling the world without a care!

Version	Issue Dates	Price Paid	Market Value
A. Yarn Antennas	Oct. 1997-May 1998		⑤ $23 ④ $26
B. Felt Antennas	June 1995-Oct. 1997		④ $150 ③ $165

Inky™

Octopus · #4028
Issued: June 25, 1994
Retired: May 1, 1998

100

Birthdate: November 29, 1994
Inky's head is big and round
As he swims he makes no sound
If you need a hand, don't hesitate
Inky can help because he has eight!

Version	Issue Dates	Price Paid	Market Value
A. Pink	June 1995-May 1998		⑤ $24 ④ $28
			③ $185
B. Tan With Mouth	Sept. 1994-June 1995		③ $625 ② $700
C. Tan Without Mouth	June 1994-Sept. 1994		② $750 ① $915

Jabber™

Parrot · #4197
Issued: May 30, 1998
Retired: December 23, 1999

101

Birthdate: October 10, 1997
Teaching Jabber to move his beak
A large vocabulary he now can speak
Jabber will repeat what you say
Teach him a new word everyday!

Version	Issue Dates	Price Paid	Market Value
Original	May 1998-Dec. 1999		⑤ $8

102

Jake™

Mallard Duck • #4199
Issued: May 30, 1998
Retired: December 23, 1999

Birthdate: April 16, 1997
Jake the drake likes to splash in a puddle
Take him home and give him a cuddle
Quack, Quack, Quack, he will say
He's so glad you're here to play!

Version	Issue Dates	Price Paid	Market Value
Original	May 1998-Dec. 1999		🏷 $8

103

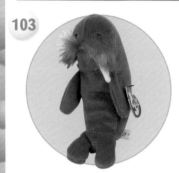

Jolly™

Walrus • #4082
Issued: May 11, 1997
Retired: May 1, 1998

Birthdate: December 2, 1996
Jolly the walrus is not very serious
He laughs and laughs until he's delirious
He often reminds me of my dad
Always happy, never sad!

Version	Issue Dates	Price Paid	Market Value
Original	May 1997-May 1998		🏷 $14 🏷 $15

104

Kicks™

Bear • #4229
Issued: January 1, 1999
Retired: December 23, 1999

Birthdate: August 16, 1998
The world cup is his dream
Kicks the bear is the best on his team
He hopes that one day he'll be the pick
First he needs to improve his kick!

Version	Issue Dates	Price Paid	Market Value
Original	Jan. 1999-Dec. 1999		🏷 $14

Page Totals	Price Paid	Market Value

COLLECTOR'S
VALUE GUIDE™

Kiwi™

Toucan · #4070
Issued: June 3, 1995
Retired: January 1, 1997

105

Birthdate: September 16, 1995
Kiwi waits for the April showers
Watching a garden bloom with flowers
There trees grow with fruit that's sweet
I'm sure you'll guess his favorite treat!

Version	Issue Dates	Price Paid	Market Value
Original	June 1995-Jan. 1997		④ $145 ③ $220

Knuckles™

Pig · #4247
Issued: April 14, 1999
Retired: December 23, 1999

106

Birthdate: March 25, 1999
In the kitchen working hard
Using ingredients from the yard
No one will eat it, can you guess why?
Her favorite recipe is for mud pie!

Version	Issue Dates	Price Paid	Market Value
Original	April 1999-Dec. 1999		⑤ $13

KuKu™

Cockatoo · #4192
Issued: May 30, 1998
Retired: December 23, 1999

107

Birthdate: January 5, 1997
This fancy bird loves to converse
He talks in poems, rhythms and verse
So take him home and give him some time
You'll be surprised how he can rhyme!

Version	Issue Dates	Price Paid	Market Value
Original	May 1998-Dec. 1999		⑤ $8

108

Lefty™
Donkey • #4085
Issued: June 15, 1996
Retired: January 1, 1997

Birthdate: July 4, 1996
Donkeys to the left, elephants to the right
Often seems like a crazy sight
This whole game seems very funny
Until you realize they're spending
Your money!

Version	Issue Dates	Price Paid	Market Value
Original	June 1996-Jan. 1997		④ $235

109

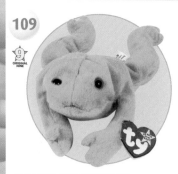

Legs™
Frog • #4020
Issued: January 8, 1994
Retired: October 1, 1997

Birthdate: April 25, 1993
Legs lives in a hollow log
Legs likes to play leap frog
If you like to hang out at the lake
Legs will be the new friend you'll make!

Version	Issue Dates	Price Paid	Market Value	
Original	Jan. 1994-Oct. 1997		④ $20 ❸ $88	❷ $310 ❶ $480

110

Libearty™
Bear • #4057
Issued: June 15, 1996
Retired: January 1, 1997

Birthdate: Summer 1996
I am called libearty
I wear the flag for all to see
Hope and freedom is my way
That's why I wear flag USA

Version	Issue Dates	Price Paid	Market Value
Original	June 1996-Jan. 1997		④ $365

Page Totals	Price Paid	Market Value

COLLECTOR'S
VALUE GUIDE™

Lips™

Fish · #4254
Issued: Summer 1999
Retired: December 23, 1999

Birthdate: March 15, 1999
Did you ever see a fish like me?
I'm the most colorful in the sea
Traveling with friends in a school
Swimming all day is really cool!

111

Version	Issue Dates	Price Paid	Market Value
Original	Summer 1999-Dec. 1999		🖐 $18

Lizzy™

Lizard · #4033
Issued: June 3, 1995
Retired: December 31, 1997

Birthdate: May 11, 1995
Lizzy loves Legs the frog
She hides with him under logs
Both of them search for flies
Underneath the clear blue skies!

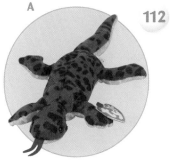

B   A

112

Version	Issue Dates	Price Paid	Market Value
A. Blue	Jan. 1996-Dec. 1997		🖐 $22 ④ $24
			③ $205
B. Tie-dye	June 1995-Jan. 1996		③ $835

Loosy™

Goose · #4206
Issued: September 30, 1998
Retired: September 1, 1999

Birthdate: March 29, 1998
A tale has been told
Of a goose that laid gold
But try as she might
Loosy's eggs are just white!

113

Version	Issue Dates	Price Paid	Market Value
Original	Sept. 1998-Sept. 1999		🖐 $10

	Price Paid	Market Value
Page Totals		

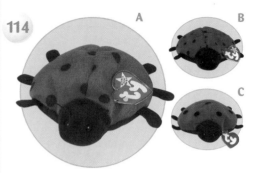

Lucky™

Ladybug • #4040
Issued: June 25, 1994
Retired: May 1, 1998

Birthdate: May 1, 1995
Lucky the lady bug loves the lotto
"Someone must win" that's her motto
But save your dimes and even a penny
Don't spend on the lotto and
You'll have many!

Version	Issue Dates	Price Paid	Market Value
A. Approx. 11 Printed Spots	Feb. 1996-May 1998		⑤ $23 ④ $23
B. Approx. 21 Printed Spots	Est. Mid 1996-Late 1996		④ $390
C. Approx. 7 Felt Glued-On Spots	June 1994-Feb. 1996		③ $215 ② $390
			① $590

Luke™

Black Lab • #4214
Issued: January 1, 1999
Retired: December 23, 1999

Birthdate: June 15, 1998
After chewing on your favorite shoes
Luke gets tired, takes a snooze
Who wouldn't love a puppy like this?
Give him a hug, he'll give you a kiss!

Version	Issue Dates	Price Paid	Market Value
Original	Jan. 1999-Dec. 1999		⑤ $11

Mac™

Cardinal • #4225
Issued: January 1, 1999
Retired: December 23, 1999

Birthdate: June 10, 1998
Mac tries hard to prove he's the best
Swinging his bat harder than the rest
Breaking records, enjoying the game
Hitting home runs is his claim to fame!

Version	Issue Dates	Price Paid	Market Value
Original	Jan. 1999-Dec. 1999		⑤ $11

Page Totals	Price Paid	Market Value

COLLECTOR'S
VALUE GUIDE™

Magic™

Dragon · #4088
Issued: June 3, 1995
Retired: December 31, 1997

B **A**

Birthdate: September 5, 1995
Magic the dragon lives in a dream
The most beautiful that you have ever seen
Through magic lands she likes to fly
Look up and watch her, way up high!

Version	Issue Dates	Price Paid	Market Value
A. Pale Pink Thread	June 1995-Dec. 1997		❹ $46 ❸ $125
B. Hot Pink Thread	Est. Mid 1996-Early 1997		❹ $80

Manny™

Manatee · #4081
Issued: January 7, 1996
Retired: May 11, 1997

Birthdate: June 8, 1995
Manny is sometimes called a sea cow
She likes to twirl and likes to bow
Manny sure is glad you bought her
Because it's so lonely under water!

Version	Issue Dates	Price Paid	Market Value
Original	Jan. 1996-May 1997		❹ $125 ❸ $200

Maple™ (exclusive to Canada)

Bear · #4600
Issued: January 1, 1997
Retired: July 30, 1999

B **A**

The
Beanie Babies
Collection™
Pride
HANDMADE IN CHINA
© 1996 TY INC.
OAKBROOK IL U.S.A.
SURFACE WASHABLE
ALL NEW MATERIAL
POLYESTER FIBER
& PVC PELLETS CE

Birthdate: July 1, 1996
Maple the bear likes to ski
With his friends, he plays hockey.
He loves his pancakes and eats every crumb
Can you guess which country he's from?

Version	Issue Dates	Price Paid	Market Value (in U.S. market)
A. "Maple™" Tush Tag	Est. Early 1997-July 1999		❺ $140 ❹ $170
B. "Pride™" Tush Tag	Est. Early 1997		❹ $450

	Price Paid	Market Value
Page Totals		

120

Mel™

Koala • #4162
Issued: January 1, 1997
Retired: March 31, 1999

Birthdate: January 15, 1996
How do you name a Koala bear?
It's rather tough, I do declare!
It confuses me, I get into a funk
I'll name him Mel, after my favorite hunk!

Version	Issue Dates	Price Paid	Market Value
Original	Jan. 1997-March 1999		⑤ $9 ④ $10

121

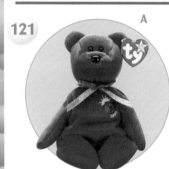

A   B

C

Millennium™

Bear • #4226
Issued: January 1, 1999
Retired: November 12, 1999

Birthdate: January 1, 1999
A brand new century has come to call
Health and happiness to one and all
Bring on the fireworks and all the fun
Let's keep the party going 'til 2001!

Version	Issue Dates	Price Paid	Market Value
A. "Millennium™" On Both Tags	Early 1999-Nov. 1999		⑤ $13
B. "Millenium™" Swing Tag & "Millennium™" Tush Tag	Early 1999		⑤ $25
C. "Millenium™" On Both Tags	Jan. 1999-Early 1999		⑤ $21

122

Mooch™

Spider Monkey • #4224
Issued: January 1, 1999
Retired: December 23, 1999

Birthdate: August 1, 1998
Look in the treetops, up towards the sky
Swinging from branches way up high
Tempt him with a banana or fruit
When he's hungry, he acts so cute!

Version	Issue Dates	Price Paid	Market Value
Original	Jan. 1999-Dec. 1999		⑤ $10

Page Totals	Price Paid	Market Value

COLLECTOR'S
VALUE GUIDE™

Morrie™

Eel · #4282
Issued: February 13, 2000
Current - Just Released

123

NEW!

Birthdate: February 20, 2000
Over, under, upside and down
Morrie loves to swim all around
He looks like a snake - could be a fish
To be your best friend is his only wish!

Version	Issue Dates	Price Paid	Market Value
Original	Feb. 2000-Current		⑥ $_____

Mystic™

Unicorn · #4007
Issued: June 25, 1994
Retired: May 18, 1999

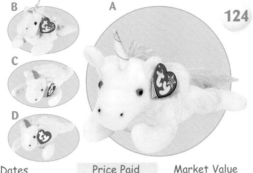

124

Birthdate: May 21, 1994
Once upon a time so far away
A unicorn was born one day in May
Keep Mystic with you, she's a prize
You'll see the magic in her blue eyes!

Version	Issue Dates	Price Paid	Market Value
A. Iridescent Horn/Fluffy Mane	Jan. 1999-May 1999		⑤ $14
B. Iridescent Horn/Coarse Mane	Oct. 1997-Dec. 1998		⑤ $11 ④ $12
C. Brown Horn/Coarse Mane	Est. Late 1995-Oct. 1997		④ $25 ③ $100
D. Brown Horn/Fine Mane	Est. June 1994-Late 1995		③ $295 ② $460
			① $550

Nana™ (name changed to "Bongo™")

Monkey · #4067
Issued: June 3, 1995
Retired: 1995

125

Birthdate: N/A
No Poem

Version	Issue Dates	Price Paid	Market Value
Original	June 1995-1995		③ $3,700

Page Totals	Price Paid	Market Value

126

Nanook™

Husky · #4104
Issued: May 11, 1997
Retired: March 31, 1999

Birthdate: November 21, 1996
Nanook is a dog that loves cold weather
To him a sled is light as a feather
Over the snow and through the slush
He runs at hearing the cry of "mush"!

Version	Issue Dates	Price Paid	Market Value
Original	May 1997-March 1999		⑤ $11 ④ $12

127

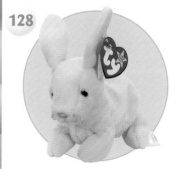

Neon™

Seahorse · #4239
Issued: April 8, 1999
Retired: December 23, 1999

Birthdate: April 1, 1999
Born in shallow water in a sea grass bay
Their eyes can swivel and look every way
Walk down the beach on a bright sunny day
Jump into the sea and watch them play!

Version	Issue Dates	Price Paid	Market Value
Original	April 1999-Dec. 1999		⑤ $12

128

Nibbler™

Rabbit · #4216
Issued: January 1, 1999
Retired: July 9, 1999

Birthdate: April 6, 1998
Twitching her nose, she looks so sweet
Small in size, she's very petite
Soft and furry, hopping with grace
She'll visit your garden, her favorite place!

Version	Issue Dates	Price Paid	Market Value
Original	Jan. 1999-July 1999		⑤ $13

Page Totals	Price Paid	Market Value

COLLECTOR'S
VALUE GUIDE™

Nibbly™

Rabbit · #4217
Issued: January 1, 1999
Retired: July 20, 1999

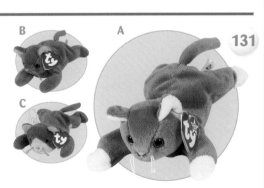

Birthdate: May 7, 1998
Wonderful ways to spend a day
Bright and sunny in the month of May
Hopping around as trees sway
Looking for friends, out to play!

Version	Issue Dates	Price Paid	Market Value
Original	Jan. 1999-July 1999		⑤ $12

Niles™

Camel · #4284
Issued: February 13, 2000
Current - Just Released

NEW!

Birthdate: February 1, 2000
The desert is a dry, hot land
Filled with lots and lots of sand
But I can still have so much fun
As long as we play in the sun!

130

Version	Issue Dates	Price Paid	Market Value
Original	Feb. 2000-Current		⑥ $_____

Nip™

Cat · #4003
Issued: January 7, 1995
Retired: December 31, 1997

131

Birthdate: March 6, 1994
His name is Nipper, but we call him Nip
His best friend is a black cat named Zip
Nip likes to run in races for fun
He runs so fast he's always number one!

Version	Issue Dates	Price Paid	Market Value	
A. White Paws	March 1996-Dec. 1997		⑤ $18	④ $18
			③ $250	
B. All Gold	Jan. 1996-March 1996		③ $840	
C. White Face	Jan. 1995-Jan. 1996		③ $480	② $540

Beanie Babies®

132

Nuts™

Squirrel • #4114
Issued: January 1, 1997
Retired: December 31, 1998

Birthdate: January 21, 1996
With his bushy tail, he'll scamper up a tree
The most cheerful critter you'll ever see,
He's nuts about nuts, and he loves to chat
Have you ever seen a squirrel like that?

Version	Issue Dates	Price Paid	Market Value
Original	Jan. 1997-Dec. 1998		⑤ $11 ④ $13

133

Osito™

(exclusive to the United States)

Bear • #4244
Issued: April 17, 1999
Retired: November 30, 1999

Birthdate: February 5, 1999
Across the waters of the Rio Grande
Lies a beautiful and mystic land
A place we all should plan to go
Known by all as Mexico!

Version	Issue Dates	Price Paid	Market Value
Original	April 1999-Nov. 1999		⑤ $25

134

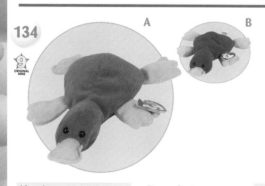

A   B

Patti™

Platypus • #4025
Issued: January 8, 1994
Retired: May 1, 1998

Birthdate: January 6, 1993
Ran into Patti one day while walking
Believe me she wouldn't stop talking
Listened and listened to her speak
That would explain her extra large beak!

Version	Issue Dates	Price Paid	Market Value
A. Magenta	Feb. 1995-May 1998		⑤ $17 ④ $21
			③ $210
B. Maroon	Jan. 1994-Feb. 1995		③ $650 ② $800
			① $900

Page Totals	Price Paid	Market Value

COLLECTOR'S
VALUE GUIDE™

Paul™

Walrus • #4248
Issued: April 12, 1999
Retired: December 23, 1999

135

Birthdate: February 23, 1999
Traveling the ocean in a submarine
Singing and playing a tambourine
One day hoping to lead a band
First he needs to find dry land!

Version	Issue Dates	Price Paid	Market Value
Original	April 1999-Dec. 1999		⑤ $12

Peace™

Bear • #4053
Issued: May 11, 1997
Retired: July 14, 1999

136

Birthdate: February 1, 1996
All races, all colors, under the sun
Join hands together and have some fun
Dance to the music, rock and roll is the sound
Symbols of peace and love abound!

Version	Issue Dates	Price Paid	Market Value
Original	May 1997-July 1999		⑤ $21 ④ $27

Peanut™

Elephant • #4062
Issued: June 3, 1995
Retired: May 1, 1998

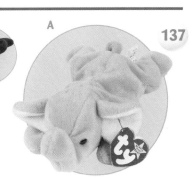

B   A

137

Birthdate: January 25, 1995
Peanut the elephant walks on tip-toes
Quietly sneaking wherever she goes
She'll sneak up on you and a hug
You will get
Peanut is a friend you won't soon forget!

Version	Issue Dates	Price Paid	Market Value
A. Light Blue	Oct. 1995-May 1998		⑤ $20 ④ $23
			③ $750
B. Dark Blue	June 1995-Oct. 1995		③ $4,400

138

Pecan™

Bear · #4251
Issued: April 8, 1999
Retired: December 23, 1999

Birthdate: April 15, 1999
In late fall, as wind gusts blow
Pecan hibernates before winter snow
In early spring, sweet scent of a flower
Wakes her up to take a shower!

Version	Issue Dates	Price Paid	Market Value
Original	April 1999-Dec. 1999		⑤ $11

139

Peking™

Panda · #4013
Issued: June 25, 1994
Retired: January 7, 1996

Birthdate: N/A
No Poem

Version	Issue Dates	Price Paid	Market Value
Original	June 1994-Jan 1996		❸ $1,600
			❷ $1,700
			❶ $2,150

140

A   B

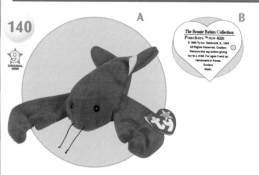

The Beanie Babies Collection
Punchers™ style 4026
© 1993 Ty Inc. Oakbrook, IL, USA
All Rights Reserved. Caution:
Remove this tag before giving
toy to a child. For ages 5 and up.
Handmade in Korea.
Surface
Wash.

Pinchers™

Lobster · #4026
Issued: January 8, 1994
Retired: May 1, 1998

Birthdate: June 19, 1993
This lobster loves to pinch
Eating his food inch by inch
Balancing carefully with his tail
Moving forward slow as a snail!

Version	Issue Dates	Price Paid	Market Value	
A. "Pinchers™" Swing Tag	Jan. 1994-May 1998		⑤ $19	④ $20
			❸ $105	❷ $390
B. "Punchers™" Swing Tag	Est. Early 1994		❶ $800	
			❶ $3,500	

	Price Paid	Market Value
Page Totals		

COLLECTOR'S
VALUE GUIDE™

Pinky™

Flamingo • #4072
Issued: June 3, 1995
Retired: December 31, 1998

Birthdate: February 13, 1995
Pinky loves the everglades
From the hottest pink she's made
With floppy legs and big orange beak
She's the Beanie that you seek!

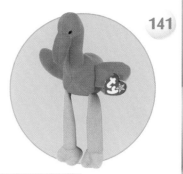

141

Version	Issue Dates	Price Paid	Market Value
Original	June 1995-Dec. 1998		❺ $10 ❹ $12
			❸ $115

Pouch™

Kangaroo • #4161
Issued: January 1, 1997
Retired: March 31, 1999

Birthdate: November 6, 1996
My little pouch is handy I've found
It helps me carry my baby around
I hop up and down without any fear
Knowing my baby is safe and near.

142

Version	Issue Dates	Price Paid	Market Value
Original	Jan. 1997-March 1999		❺ $9 ❹ $11

Pounce™

Cat • #4122
Issued: December 31, 1997
Retired: March 31, 1999

Birthdate: August 28, 1997
Sneaking and slinking down the hall
To pounce upon a fluffy yarn ball
Under the tables, around the chairs
Through the rooms and down the stairs!

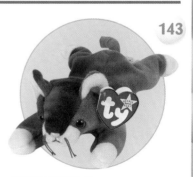

143

Version	Issue Dates	Price Paid	Market Value
Original	Dec. 1997-March 1999		❺ $9

144

Prance™

Cat • #4123
Issued: December 31, 1997
Retired: March 31, 1999

Birthdate: November 20, 1997
She darts around and swats the air
Then looks confused when nothing's there
Pick her up and pet her soft fur
Listen closely, and you'll hear her purr!

Version	Issue Dates	Price Paid	Market Value
Original	Dec. 1997-March 1999		$9

145

Prickles™

Hedgehog • #4220
Issued: January 1, 1999
Retired: December 23, 1999

Birthdate: February 19, 1998
Prickles the hedgehog loves to play
She rolls around the meadow all day
Tucking under her feet and head
Suddenly she looks like a ball instead!

Version	Issue Dates	Price Paid	Market Value
Original	Jan. 1999-Dec. 1999		$10

146

Princess™

Bear • #4300
Issued: October 29, 1997
Retired: April 13, 1999

Birthdate: N/A
Like an angel, she came from heaven above
She shared her compassion, her pain, her love
She only stayed with us long enough to teach
The world to share, to give, to reach.

Version	Issue Dates	Price Paid	Market Value
A. "P.E. Pellets" On Tush Tag	Est. Late 1997-April 1999		$23
B. "P.V.C. Pellets" On Tush Tag	Est. Late 1997		$95

Page Totals	Price Paid	Market Value

COLLECTOR'S
VALUE GUIDE™

Puffer™
Puffin · #4181
Issued: December 31, 1997
Retired: September 18, 1998

147

Birthdate: November 3, 1997
What in the world does a puffin do?
We're sure that you would like to know too
We asked Puffer how she spends her days
Before she answered, she flew away!

Version	Issue Dates	Price Paid	Market Value
Original	Dec. 1997-Sept. 1998		🌀 $10

Pugsly™
Pug Dog · #4106
Issued: May 11, 1997
Retired: March 31, 1999

148

Birthdate: May 2, 1996
Pugsly is picky about what he will wear
Never a spot, a stain or a tear
Image is something of which he'll gloat
Until he noticed his wrinkled coat!

Version	Issue Dates	Price Paid	Market Value
Original	May 1997-March 1999		🌀 $10 ④ $11

Pumkin'™
Pumpkin · #4205
Issued: September 30, 1998
Retired: December 31, 1998

149

Birthdate: October 31, 1998
Ghost and goblins are out tonight
Witches try hard to cause fright
This little pumpkin is very sweet
He only wants to trick or treat!

Version	Issue Dates	Price Paid	Market Value
Original	Sept. 1998-Dec. 1998		🌀 $25

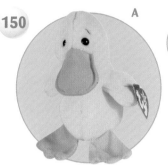

Quackers™
Duck • #4024
Issued: June 25, 1994
Retired: May 1, 1998

Birthdate: April 19, 1994
There is a duck by the name of Quackers
Every night he eats animal crackers
He swims in a lake that's clear and blue
But he'll come to the shore to be with you!

Version	Issue Dates	Price Paid	Market Value	
A. "Quackers™" With Wings	Jan. 1995-May 1998		⑤ $13	④ $15
B. "Quacker™" Without Wings	June 1994-Jan. 1995		❸ $85	❷ $600
			❷ $1,900	❶ $2,300

Radar™
Bat • #4091
Issued: September 1, 1995
Retired: May 11, 1997

Birthdate: October 30, 1995
Radar the bat flies late at night
He can soar to an amazing height
If you see something as high as a star
Take a good look, it might be Radar!

Version	Issue Dates	Price Paid	Market Value	
Original	Sept. 1995-May 1997		④ $130	❸ $195

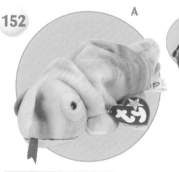

Rainbow™
Chameleon • #4037
Issued: December 31, 1997
Retired: March 31, 1999

Birthdate: October 14, 1997
Red, green, blue and yellow
This chameleon is a colorful fellow.
A blend of colors, his own unique hue
Rainbow was made especially for you!

Version	Issue Dates	Price Paid	Market Value
A. Tie-dye/With Tongue	Mid 1998-March 1999		⑤ $13
B. Blue/No Tongue	Dec. 1997-Mid 1998		⑤ $13

	Price Paid	Market Value
Page Totals		

COLLECTOR'S
VALUE GUIDE™

Rex™

Tyrannosaurus • #4086
Issued: June 3, 1995
Retired: June 15, 1996

Birthdate: N/A
No Poem

153

Version	Issue Dates	Price Paid	Market Value
Original	June 1995-June 1996		③ $700

Righty™

Elephant • #4086
Issued: June 15, 1996
Retired: January 1, 1997

Birthdate: July 4, 1996
Donkeys to the left, elephants to the right
Often seems like a crazy sight
This whole game seems very funny
Until you realize they're spending
Your money!

154

Version	Issue Dates	Price Paid	Market Value
Original	June 1996-Jan. 1997		④ $235

Ringo™

Raccoon • #4014
Issued: January 7, 1996
Retired: September 16, 1998

Birthdate: July 14, 1995
Ringo hides behind his mask
He will come out, if you should ask
He loves to chitter. He loves to chatter
Just about anything, it doesn't matter!

155

Version	Issue Dates	Price Paid	Market Value
Original	Jan. 1996-Sept. 1998		⑤ $12 ④ $14
			③ $80

156

Roam™

Buffalo • #4209
Issued: September 30, 1998
Retired: December 23, 1999

Birthdate: September 27, 1998
Once roaming wild on American land
Tall and strong, wooly and grand
So rare and special is this guy
Find him quickly, he's quite a buy!

Version	Issue Dates	Price Paid	Market Value
Original	Sept. 1998-Dec. 1999		💲 $9

157

Roary™

Lion • #4069
Issued: May 11, 1997
Retired: December 31, 1998

Birthdate: February 20, 1996
Deep in the jungle they crowned him king
But being brave is not his thing
A cowardly lion some may say
He hears his roar and runs away!

Version	Issue Dates	Price Paid	Market Value
Original	May 1997-Dec. 1998		💲 $11 💲 $12

158

Rocket™

Blue Jay • #4202
Issued: May 30, 1998
Retired: December 23, 1999

Birthdate: March 12, 1997
Rocket is the fastest blue jay ever
He flies in all sorts of weather
Aerial tricks are his specialty
He's so entertaining for you and me!

Version	Issue Dates	Price Paid	Market Value
Original	May 1998-Dec. 1999		💲 $8

Page Totals	Price Paid	Market Value

COLLECTOR'S
VALUE GUIDE™

Rover™

Dog · #4101
Issued: June 15, 1996
Retired: May 1, 1998

Birthdate: May 30, 1996
This dog is red and his name is Rover
If you call him he is sure to come over
He barks and plays with all his might
But worry not, he won't bite!

159

Version	Issue Dates	Price Paid	Market Value
Original	June 1996-May 1998		🏐 $19 ④ $21

Rufus™

Dog · #4280
Issued: February 13, 2000
Current - Just Released

Birthdate: February 28, 2000
Smart and friendly as can be
I'm really cute as you can see
Play with me, we'll have some fun
Throw a ball and watch me run!

160

NEW!

Version	Issue Dates	Price Paid	Market Value
Original	Feb. 2000-Current		⑥ $_____

Sakura™ さくら™

(exclusive to Japan)

Bear · #4602
Issued: March 17, 2000
Current - Just Released

Birthdate: March 25, 2000

わたしは日本の宝物
あなたに春と愛を運んでくるよ
抱きしめられたら心が暖まって
ほら、花が咲いた

Poem Translation

I am a Japanese treasure.
I will bring Spring and love to you.
When you hug me, my heart gets warm,
And look! The flower has blossomed.

161

NEW!

Version	Issue Dates	Price Paid	Market Value
Original	March 2000-Current		⑥ $_____

Page Totals	Price Paid	Market Value

162

Sammy™

Bear • #4215
Issued: January 1, 1999
Retired: December 23, 1999

Birthdate: June 23, 1998
As Sammy steps up to the plate
The crowd gets excited, can hardly wait
We know Sammy won't let us down
He makes us the happiest fans in town!

Version	Issue Dates	Price Paid	Market Value
Original	Jan. 1999-Dec. 1999		$11

163

Santa™

Santa • #4203
Issued: September 30, 1998
Retired: December 31, 1998

Birthdate: December 6, 1998
Known by all in his suit of red
Piles of presents on his sled
Generous and giving, he brings us joy
Peace and love, plus this special toy!

Version	Issue Dates	Price Paid	Market Value
Original	Sept. 1998-Dec. 1998		$30

164

NEW!

Sarge™

German Shepherd • #4277
Issued: February 13, 2000
Current - Just Released

Birthdate: February 14, 2000
I defend you, so count on me
To stay by your side, that's where I'll be
Protect and serve is what I do
For just a little hug from you!

Version	Issue Dates	Price Paid	Market Value
Original	Feb. 2000-Current		$_____

Page Totals	Price Paid	Market Value

COLLECTOR'S
VALUE GUIDE™

Scaly™
165

Lizard · #4263
Issued: August 31, 1999
Retired: December 23, 1999

Birthdate: February 9, 1999
I love to lie, basking in the sun
Living in the desert sure is fun
Climbing up cactus, avoiding a spike
I'm the Beanie you're sure to like!

Version	Issue Dates	Price Paid	Market Value
Original	Aug. 1999-Dec. 1999		🌀 $10

Scat™
166

Cat · #4231
Issued: January 1, 1999
Retired: December 23, 1999

Birthdate: May 27, 1998
Newborn kittens require lots of sleep
Shhh . . . it's naptime, don't make a peep
Touch her fur, it feels like silk
Wake her up to drink mother's milk!

Version	Issue Dates	Price Paid	Market Value
Original	Jan. 1999-Dec. 1999		🌀 $10

Schweetheart™
167

Orangutan · #4252
Issued: April 11, 1999
Retired: December 23, 1999

Birthdate: January 23, 1999
Of all the jungles filled with vines
Traveling about, you came to mine
Because of all the things you said
I can't seem to get you outta my head!

Version	Issue Dates	Price Paid	Market Value
Original	April 1999-Dec. 1999		🌀 $11

	Price Paid	Market Value
Page Totals		

168

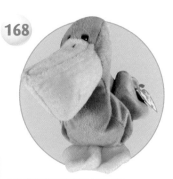

Scoop™
Pelican · #4107
Issued: June 15, 1996
Retired: December 31, 1998

Birthdate: July 1, 1996
All day long he scoops up fish
To fill his bill, is his wish
Diving fast and diving low
Hoping those fish are very slow!

Version	Issue Dates	Price Paid	Market Value
Original	June 1996-Dec. 1998		⑤ $11 ④ $12

169

Scorch™
Dragon · #4210
Issued: September 30, 1998
Retired: December 23, 1999

Birthdate: July 31, 1998
A magical mystery with glowing wings
Made by wizards and other things
Known to breathe fire with lots of smoke
Scorch is really a friendly ol' bloke!

Version	Issue Dates	Price Paid	Market Value
Original	Sept. 1998-Dec. 1999		⑤ $10

170

Scottie™
Scottish Terrier · #4102
Issued: June 15, 1996
Retired: May 1, 1998

Birthdate: June 3, 1996
or June 15, 1996
Scottie is a friendly sort
Even though his legs are short
He is always happy as can be
His best friends are you and me!

Version	Issue Dates	Price Paid	Market Value
Original	June 1996-May 1998		⑤ $21 ④ $23

Page Totals	Price Paid	Market Value

COLLECTOR'S
VALUE GUIDE™

Scurry™

Beetle · #4281
Issued: February 13, 2000
Current - Just Released

NEW!

Birthdate: January 18, 2000
I play in the cellar with all of my friends
We laugh, we sing, the fun never ends
I hurry and scurry and hide most of the day
But if you come down, I'll stay out and play!

171

Version	Issue Dates	Price Paid	Market Value
Original	Feb. 2000-Current		**6** $_____

Seamore™

Seal · #4029
Issued: June 25, 1994
Retired: October 1, 1997

Birthdate: December 14, 1996
Seamore is a little white seal
Fish and clams are her favorite meal
Playing and laughing in the sand
She's the happiest seal in the land!

172

Version	Issue Dates	Price Paid	Market Value
Original	June 1994-Oct. 1997		**4** $110 **3** $185 **2** $400 **1** $620

Seaweed™

Otter · #4080
Issued: January 7, 1996
Retired: September 19, 1998

Birthdate: March 19, 1996
Seaweed is what she likes to eat
It's supposed to be a delicious treat
Have you tried a treat from the water
If you haven't, maybe you "otter"!

173

Version	Issue Dates	Price Paid	Market Value
Original	Jan. 1996-Sept. 1998		**5** $20 **4** $23 **3** $85

174

Sheets™

Ghost • #4260
Issued: August 31, 1999
Retired: December 23, 1999

Birthdate: October 31, 1999
Living alone in a haunted house
Friend to the spider, bat and mouse
Often heard, but never seen
Waiting to wish you "Happy Halloween!"

Version	Issue Dates	Price Paid	Market Value
Original	Aug. 1999-Dec. 1999		🪙 $12

175

Silver™

Cat • #4242
Issued: April 21, 1999
Retired: December 23, 1999

Birthdate: February 11, 1999
Curled up, sleeping in the sun
He's worn out from having fun
Chasing dust specks in the sunrays
This is how he spends his days!

Version	Issue Dates	Price Paid	Market Value
Original	April 1999-Dec. 1999		🪙 $11

176

Slippery™

Seal • #4222
Issued: January 1, 1999
Retired: December 23, 1999

Birthdate: January 17, 1998
In the ocean, near a breaking wave
Slippery the seal acts very brave
On his surfboard, he sees a swell
He's riding the wave! Oooops . . . he fell!

Version	Issue Dates	Price Paid	Market Value
Original	Jan. 1999-Dec. 1999		🪙 $9

Page Totals	Price Paid	Market Value

COLLECTOR'S
VALUE GUIDE™

Slither™
177

Snake · #4031
Issued: June 25, 1994
Retired: June 15, 1995

Birthdate: N/A
No Poem

Version	Issue Dates	Price Paid	Market Value
Original	June 1994-June 1995		❸ $1,550 ❷ $1,750 ❶ $2,050

Slowpoke™
178

Sloth · #4261
Issued: August 31, 1999
Retired: December 23, 1999

Birthdate: May 20, 1999
Look up in the sky to the top of the tree
What in the world is that you see?
A little sloth as sweet as can be
Munching on leaves very slowly!

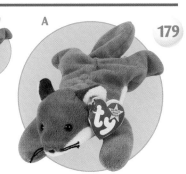

Version	Issue Dates	Price Paid	Market Value
Original	Aug. 1999-Dec. 1999		❺ $10

Sly™
179

Fox · #4115
Issued: June 15, 1996
Retired: September 22, 1998

Birthdate: September 12, 1996
Sly is a fox and tricky is he
Please don't chase him, let him be
If you want him, just say when
He'll peek out from his den!

Version	Issue Dates	Price Paid	Market Value
A. White Belly	Aug. 1996-Sept. 1998		❺ $12 ❹ $14
B. Brown Belly	June 1996-Aug. 1996		❹ $130

180

Smoochy™
Frog • #4039
Issued: December 31, 1997
Retired: March 31, 1999

Birthdate: October 1, 1997
Is he a frog or maybe a prince?
This confusion makes him wince
Find the answer, help him with this
Be the one to give him a kiss!

Version	Issue Dates	Price Paid	Market Value
Original	Dec. 1997-March 1999		$10

181

NEW!

Sneaky™
Leopard • #4278
Issued: February 13, 2000
Current - Just Released

Birthdate: February 22, 2000
A shadow in the dark you'll see
Don't be afraid, it's only me
My spots will hide me 'til I see
That you are just the friend for me!

Version	Issue Dates	Price Paid	Market Value
Original	Feb. 2000-Current		$_____

182

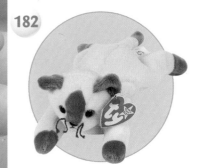

Snip™
Siamese Cat • #4120
Issued: January 1, 1997
Retired: December 31, 1998

Birthdate: October 22, 1996
Snip the cat is Siamese
She'll be your friend if you please
So toss her a toy or a piece of string
Playing with you is her favorite thing!

Version	Issue Dates	Price Paid	Market Value
Original	Jan. 1997-Dec. 1998		$11 $12

Page Totals	Price Paid	Market Value

COLLECTOR'S
VALUE GUIDE™

Snort™

Bull • #4002
Issued: January 1, 1997
Retired: September 15, 1998

Birthdate: May 15, 1995
Although Snort is not so tall
He loves to play basketball
He is a star player in his dreams
Can you guess his favorite team?

183

Version	Issue Dates	Price Paid	Market Value
Original	Jan. 1997-Sept. 1998		⑤ $12 ④ $13

Snowball™

Snowman • #4201
Issued: October 1, 1997
Retired: December 31, 1997

Birthdate: December 22, 1996
There is a snowman, I've been told
That plays with Beanies out in the cold
What is better in a winter wonderland
Than a Beanie snowman in your hand!

184

Version	Issue Dates	Price Paid	Market Value
Original	Oct. 1997-Dec. 1997		④ $36

Spangle™

Bear • #4245
Issued: April 24, 1999
Retired: December 23, 1999

Birthdate: June 14, 1999
Stars and stripes he wears proudly
Everywhere he goes he says loudly
"Hip hip hooray, for the land of the free
There's no place on earth I'd rather be!"

185

Version	Issue Dates	Price Paid	Market Value
A. Blue Face	April 1999-Dec. 1999		⑤ $48
B. Red Face	April 1999-Dec. 1999		⑤ $25
C. White Face	April 1999-Dec. 1999		⑤ $35

	Price Paid	Market Value
Page Totals		

186

Sparky™
Dalmatian • #4100
Issued: June 15, 1996
Retired: May 11, 1997

Birthdate: February 27, 1996
Sparky rides proud on the fire truck
Ringing the bell and pushing his luck
He gets under foot when trying to help
He often gets stepped on and
Lets out a yelp!

Version	Issue Dates	Price Paid	Market Value
Original	June 1996-May 1997		❹ $115

187

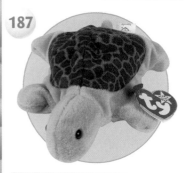

Speedy™
Turtle • #4030
Issued: June 25, 1994
Retired: October 1, 1997

Birthdate: August 14, 1994
Speedy ran marathons in the past
Such a shame, always last
Now Speedy is a big star
After he bought a racing car!

Version	Issue Dates	Price Paid	Market Value	
Original	June 1994-Oct. 1997		❹ $28	❸ $95
			❷ $280	❶ $480

188

Spike™
Rhinoceros • #4060
Issued: June 15, 1996
Retired: December 31, 1998

Birthdate: August 13, 1996
Spike the rhino likes to stampede
He's the bruiser that you need
Gentle to birds on his back and spike
You can be his friend if you like!

Version	Issue Dates	Price Paid	Market Value	
Original	June 1996-Dec. 1998		❺ $9	❹ $10

	Price Paid	Market Value
Page Totals		

COLLECTOR'S
VALUE GUIDE™

Spinner™

Spider • #4036
Issued: October 1, 1997
Retired: September 19, 1998

189

Birthdate: October 28, 1996
Does this spider make you scared?
Among many people that feeling is shared
Remember spiders have feelings too
In fact, this spider really likes you!

Version	Issue Dates	Price Paid	Market Value
A. "Spinner™" Tush Tag	Oct. 1997-Sept. 1998		⑤ $11 ④ $13
B. "Creepy™" Tush Tag	Est. Late 1997-Sept. 1998		⑤ $65

Splash™

Whale • #4022
Issued: January 8, 1994
Retired: May 11, 1997

190

Birthdate: July 8, 1993
Splash loves to jump and dive
He's the fastest whale alive
He always wins the 100 yard dash
With a victory jump he'll make a splash!

Version	Issue Dates	Price Paid	Market Value
Original	Jan. 1994-May 1997		④ $110 ③ $160
			② $380 ① $575

Spooky™

Ghost • #4090
Issued: September 1, 1995
Retired: December 31, 1997

191

Birthdate: October 31, 1995
Ghosts can be a scary sight
But don't let Spooky bring you any fright
Because when you're alone, you will see
The best friend that Spooky can be!

Version	Issue Dates	Price Paid	Market Value
A. "Spooky™" Swing Tag	Est. Late 1995-Dec. 1997		④ $29 ③ $125
B. "Spook™" Swing Tag	Est. Sept. 1995-Late 1995		③ $455

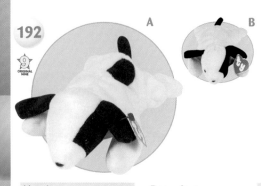

192

A B

Spot™
Dog · #4000
Issued: January 8, 1994
Retired: October 1, 1997

Birthdate: January 3, 1993
See Spot sprint, see Spot run
You and Spot will have lots of fun
Watch out now, because he's not slow
Just stand back and watch him go!

Version	Issue Dates	Price Paid	Market Value
A. With Spot	April 1994-Oct. 1997		❹ $48 ❸ $125
			❷ $650
B. Without Spot	Jan. 1994-April 1994		❷ $1,750 ❶ $2,250

193

NEW!

Springy™
Bunny · #4272
Issued: February 13, 2000
Current - Just Released

Birthdate: February 29, 2000
Hopping and jumping all around
I never stay long on the ground
I might be gone for just a while
But I'll be back and make you smile!

Version	Issue Dates	Price Paid	Market Value
Original	Feb. 2000-Current		❻ $_____

194

Spunky™
Cocker Spaniel · #4184
Issued: December 31, 1997
Retired: March 31, 1999

Birthdate: January 14, 1997
Bouncing around without much grace
To jump on your lap and lick your face
But watch him closely he has no fears
He'll run so fast he'll trip over his ears

Version	Issue Dates	Price Paid	Market Value
Original	Dec. 1997-March 1999		❺ $10

Page Totals	Price Paid	Market Value

COLLECTOR'S
VALUE GUIDE™

Squealer™

Pig · #4005
Issued: January 8, 1994
Retired: May 1, 1998

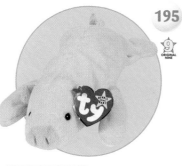

Birthdate: April 23, 1993
Squealer likes to joke around
He is known as class clown
Listen to his stories awhile
There is no doubt he'll make you smile!

195

Version	Issue Dates	Price Paid	Market Value
Original	Jan. 1994-May 1998		⑤ $24 ④ $26
			③ $82 ② $270
			① $540

Steg™

Stegosaurus · #4087
Issued: June 3, 1995
Retired: June 15, 1996

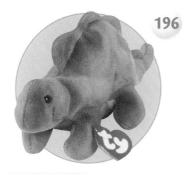

Birthdate: N/A
No Poem

196

Version	Issue Dates	Price Paid	Market Value
Original	June 1995-June 1996		③ $750

Stilts™

Stork · #4221
Issued: January 1, 1999
Retired: May 31, 1999

Birthdate: June 16, 1998
Flying high over mountains and streams
Fulfilling wishes, hopes and dreams
The stork brings parents bundles of joy
The greatest gift, a girl or boy!

197

Version	Issue Dates	Price Paid	Market Value
Original	Jan. 1999-May 1999		⑤ $10

	Price Paid	Market Value
Page Totals		

198

Sting™
Stingray • #4077
Issued: June 3, 1995
Retired: January 1, 1997

Birthdate: August 27, 1995
I'm a manta ray and my name is Sting
I'm quite unusual and this is the thing
Under the water I glide like a bird
Have you ever seen something so absurd?

Version	Issue Dates	Price Paid	Market Value
Original	June 1995-Jan. 1997		❹ $140 ❸ $235

199

Stinger™
Scorpion • #4193
Issued: May 30, 1998
Retired: December 31, 1998

Birthdate: September 29, 1997
Stinger the scorpion will run and dart
But this little fellow is really all heart
So if you see him don't run away
Say hello and ask him to play!

Version	Issue Dates	Price Paid	Market Value
Original	May 1998-Dec. 1998		❺ $10

200

Stinky™
Skunk • #4017
Issued: June 3, 1995
Retired: September 28, 1998

Birthdate: February 13, 1995
Deep in the woods he lived in a cave
Perfume and mints were the gifts he gave
He showered every night in the kitchen sink
Hoping one day he wouldn't stink!

Version	Issue Dates	Price Paid	Market Value
Original	June 1995-Sept. 1998		❺ $13 ❹ $15
			❸ $85

Page Totals	Price Paid	Market Value

COLLECTOR'S
VALUE GUIDE™

Stretch™

Ostrich • #4182
Issued: December 31, 1997
Retired: March 31, 1999

Birthdate: September 21, 1997
She thinks when her head is underground
The rest of her body can't be found
The Beanie Babies think it's absurd
To play hide and seek with this bird!

201

Version	Issue Dates	Price Paid	Market Value
Original	Dec. 1997-March 1999		❺ $11

Stripes™

Tiger • #4065
Issued: Est. June 3, 1995
Retired: May 1, 1998

Birthdate: June 11, 1995
Stripes was never fierce nor strong
So with tigers, he didn't get along
Jungle life was hard to get by
So he came to his friends at Ty!

202

Version	Issue Dates	Price Paid	Market Value
A. Light w/Fewer Stripes	June 1996-May 1998		❺ $14 ❹ $16
B. Dark w/Fuzzy Belly	Est. Early 1996-June 1996		❸ $800
C. Dark w/More Stripes	Est. June 1995-Early 1996		❸ $375

Strut™ (name changed from "Doodle™")

Rooster • #4171
Issued: July 12, 1997
Retired: March 31, 1999

Birthdate: March 8, 1996
Listen closely to "cock-a-doodle-doo"
What's the rooster saying to you?
Hurry, wake up sleepy head
We have lots to do, get out of bed!

203

Version	Issue Dates	Price Paid	Market Value
Original	July 1997-March 1999		❺ $10 ❹ $12

Page Totals	Price Paid	Market Value

204

NEW!

Swampy™
Alligator · #4273
Issued: February 13, 2000
Current - Just Released

Birthdate: January 24, 2000
Through the murky swamps I glide
My yellow eyes I try to hide
I drift as silent as a log
A friend to you and every frog!

Version	Issue Dates	Price Paid	Market Value
Original	Feb. 2000-Current		$\textcircled{6}$ $_____

205

Swirly™
Snail · #4249
Issued: April 14, 1999
Retired: December 23, 1999

Birthdate: March 10, 1999
Carefully traveling, leaving a trail
I'm not very fast, for I am a snail
Although I go my own plodding pace
Slow and steady, wins the race!

Version	Issue Dates	Price Paid	Market Value
Original	April 1999-Dec. 1999		$\textcircled{5}$ $12

206

NEW!

Swoop™
Pterodactyl · #4268
Issued: February 13, 2000
Current - Just Released

Birthdate: February 24, 2000
Gliding through the summer sky
Looking low and looking high
Now I think my quest can end
I've found you, my special friend!

Version	Issue Dates	Price Paid	Market Value
Original	Feb. 2000-Current		$\textcircled{6}$ $_____

Page Totals	Price Paid	Market Value

COLLECTOR'S
VALUE GUIDE™

Tabasco™

Bull · #4002
Issued: June 3, 1995
Retired: January 1, 1997

207

Birthdate: May 15, 1995
Although Tabasco is not so tall
He loves to play basketball
He is a star player in his dream
Can you guess his favorite team?

Version	Issue Dates	Price Paid	Market Value
Original	June 1995-Jan. 1997		❹ $140　❸ $210

Tank™

Armadillo · #4031
Issued: Est. January 7, 1996
Retired: October 1, 1997

208

Birthdate: February 22, 1995
This armadillo lives in the South
Shoving Tex-Mex in his mouth
He sure loves it south of the border
Keeping his friends in good order!

Version	Issue Dates	Price Paid	Market Value
A. 9 Plates/With Shell	Est. Late 1996-Oct. 1997		❹ $65
B. 9 Plates/Without Shell	Est. Mid 1996-Late 1996		❹ $280
C. 7 Plates/Without Shell	Est. Jan. 1996-Mid 1996		❸ $195

Teddy™ (brown)

Bear · #4050
Issued: June 25, 1994
Retired: October 1, 1997

209

Birthdate: November 28, 1995
Teddy wanted to go out today
All of his friends went out to play
But he'd rather help whatever you do
After all, his best friend is you!

Version	Issue Dates	Price Paid	Market Value
A. New Face	Jan. 1995-Oct. 1997		❹ $90　❸ $350 ❷ $775
B. Old Face	June 1994-Jan. 1995		❷ $2,300　❶ $2,500

Page Totals	Price Paid	Market Value

210

A
B

Teddy™ (cranberry)

Bear • #4052
Issued: June 25, 1994
Retired: January 7, 1996

Birthdate: N/A
No Poem

Version	Issue Dates	Price Paid	Market Value
A. New Face	Jan. 1995-Jan. 1996		❸ $1,600 ❷ $1,800
B. Old Face	June 1994-Jan. 1995		❷ $1,600 ❶ $1,800

211

A
B

Teddy™ (jade)

Bear • #4057
Issued: June 25, 1994
Retired: January 7, 1996

Birthdate: N/A
No Poem

Version	Issue Dates	Price Paid	Market Value
A. New Face	Jan. 1995-Jan. 1996		❸ $1,600 ❷ $1,800
B. Old Face	June 1994-Jan. 1995		❷ $1,600 ❶ $1,800

212

A
B

Teddy™ (magenta)

Bear • #4056
Issued: June 25, 1994
Retired: January 7, 1996

Birthdate: N/A
No Poem

Version	Issue Dates	Price Paid	Market Value
A. New Face	Jan. 1995-Jan. 1996		❸ $1,600 ❷ $1,800
B. Old Face	June 1994-Jan. 1995		❷ $1,600 ❶ $1,800

Page Totals	Price Paid	Market Value

COLLECTOR'S
VALUE GUIDE™

Teddy™ (teal)

Bear · #4051
Issued: June 25, 1994
Retired: January 7, 1996

Birthdate: N/A
No Poem

213

Version	Issue Dates	Price Paid	Market Value
A. New Face	Jan. 1995-Jan. 1996		③ $1,600 ❷ $1,800
B. Old Face	June 1994-Jan. 1995		❷ $1,600 ❶ $1,800

Teddy™ (violet)

Bear · #4055
Issued: June 25, 1994
Retired: January 7, 1996

Birthdate: N/A
No Poem

214

Version	Issue Dates	Price Paid	Market Value
A. New Face	Jan. 1995-Jan. 1996		③ $1,600 ❷ $1,800
B. New Face/Employee Bear, Red Tush Tag (Green or Red Ribbon)	Sept. 1996		No Swing Tag $3,800
C. Old Face	June 1994-Jan. 1995		❷ $1,600 ❶ $1,800

The Beginning™

Bear · #4267
Issued: February 13, 2000
Current - Just Released

Birthdate: January 1, 2000
Beanie Babies can never end
They'll always be our special friends
Start the fun because we're here
To bring you hope, love and cheer!

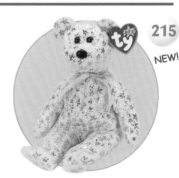

215

NEW!

Version	Issue Dates	Price Paid	Market Value
Original	Feb. 2000-Current		⑥ $_____

Page Totals	Price Paid	Market Value

216

The End™
Bear • #4265
Issued: August 31, 1999
Retired: December 23, 1999

Birthdate: N/A
All good things come to an end
It's been fun for everyone
Peace and hope are never gone
Love you all and say, "So long!"

Version	Issue Dates	Price Paid	Market Value
Original	Aug. 1999-Dec. 1999		💲 $40

217

Tiny™
Chihuahua • #4234
Issued: January 1, 1999
Retired: December 23, 1999

Birthdate: September 8, 1998
South of the Border, in the sun
Tiny the Chihuahua is having fun
Attending fiestas, breaking piñatas
Eating a taco, or some enchiladas!

Version	Issue Dates	Price Paid	Market Value
Original	Jan. 1999-Dec. 1999		💲 $11

218

Tiptoe™
Mouse • #4241
Issued: April 16, 1999
Retired: October 21, 1999

Birthdate: January 8, 1999
Creeping quietly along the wall
Little foot prints fast and small
Tiptoeing through the house with ease
Searching for a piece of cheese!

Version	Issue Dates	Price Paid	Market Value
Original	Apr. 1999-Oct. 1999		💲 $12

Page Totals	Price Paid	Market Value

COLLECTOR'S
VALUE GUIDE™

Tracker™

Basset Hound • #4198
Issued: May 30, 1998
Retired: November 26, 1999

Birthdate: June 5, 1997
Sniffing and tracking and following trails
Tracker the basset always wags his tail
It doesn't matter what you do
He's always happy when he's with you!

219

Version	Issue Dates	Price Paid	Market Value
Original	May 1998-Nov. 1999		⑤ $9

Trap™

Mouse • #4042
Issued: June 25, 1994
Retired: June 15, 1995

Birthdate: N/A
No Poem

220

Version	Issue Dates	Price Paid	Market Value
Original	June 1994-June 1995		❸ $1,150 ❷ $1,450 ❶ $1,750

Trumpet™

Elephant • #4276
Issued: February 13, 2000
Current - Just Released

Birthdate: February 11, 2000
Trumpet uses his trunk to spray
Be careful you don't get in his way
He plays in mud – he never forgets
Give him some peanuts, he'll be your pet!

221

NEW!

Version	Issue Dates	Price Paid	Market Value
Original	Feb. 2000-Current		❻ $_____

222

Tuffy™

Terrier • #4108
Issued: May 11, 1997
Retired: December 31, 1998

Birthdate: October 12, 1996
Taking off with a thunderous blast
Tuffy rides his motorcycle fast
The Beanies roll with laughs and squeals
He never took off his training wheels!

Version	Issue Dates	Price Paid	Market Value
Original	May 1997-Dec. 1998		⑤ $11 ④ $13

223

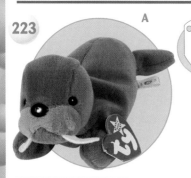

A

B

Tuck™ style 4076
DATE OF BIRTH: 9-18-95

Tusk brushes his teeth everyday
To keep them shiny, it's the only way
Teeth are special, so you must try
And they will sparkle when
You say "Hi"!

Visit our web page!!!
http://www.ty.com

Tusk™

Walrus • #4076
Issued: Est. June 3, 1995
Retired: January 1, 1997

Birthdate: September 18, 1995
Tusk brushes his teeth everyday
To keep them shiny, it's the only way
Teeth are special, so you must try
And they will sparkle when
You say "Hi"!

Version	Issue Dates	Price Paid	Market Value
A. "Tusk™" Swing Tag	Est. June 1995-Jan. 1997		④ $115 ③ $180
B. "Tuck™" Swing Tag	Est. Early 1996-Jan. 1997		④ $130

224

Twigs™

Giraffe • #4068
Issued: January 7, 1996
Retired: May 1, 1998

Birthdate: May 19, 1995
Twigs has his head in the clouds
He stands tall, he stands proud
With legs so skinny they wobble and shake
What an unusual friend he will make!

Version	Issue Dates	Price Paid	Market Value
Original	Jan. 1996-May 1998		⑤ $20 ④ $22
			③ $90

Page Totals	Price Paid	Market Value

COLLECTOR'S
VALUE GUIDE™

Ty 2K™

Bear • #4262
Issued: August 31, 1999
Retired: December 23, 1999

Birthdate: January 1, 2000
Red, yellow, green and blue
Let's have some fun me and you
So join the party, and let's all say
"Happy New Millennium", from Ty 2K!

Version	Issue Dates	Price Paid	Market Value
Original	Aug. 1999-Dec. 1999		5 $32

Valentina™

Bear • #4233
Issued: January 1, 1999
Retired: December 23, 1999

Birthdate: February 14, 1998
Flowers, candy and hearts galore
Sweet words of love for those you adore
With this bear comes love that's true
On Valentine's Day and all year through!

226

Version	Issue Dates	Price Paid	Market Value
Original	Jan. 1999-Dec. 1999		5 $14

Valentino™

Bear • #4058
Issued: January 7, 1995
Retired: December 31, 1998

Birthdate: February 14, 1994
His heart is red and full of love
He cares for you so give him a hug
Keep him close when feeling blue
Feel the love he has for you!

227

Version	Issue Dates	Price Paid	Market Value	
Original	Jan. 1995-Dec. 1998		5 $22	4 $26
			3 $145	2 $300

228

Velvet™

Panther • #4064
Issued: June 3, 1995
Retired: October 1, 1997

Birthdate: December 16, 1995
Velvet loves to sleep in the trees
Lulled to dreams by the buzz of the bees
She snoozes all day and plays all night
Running and jumping in the moonlight!

Version	Issue Dates	Price Paid	Market Value
Original	June 1995-Oct. 1997		④ $30 ③ $95

229

Waddle™

Penguin • #4075
Issued: June 3, 1995
Retired: May 1, 1998

Birthdate: December 19, 1995
Waddle the Penguin likes to dress up
Every night he wears his tux
When Waddle walks, it never fails
He always trips over his tails!

Version	Issue Dates	Price Paid	Market Value
Original	June 1995-May 1998		⑤ $21 ④ $23 ③ $90

230

Wallace™

Bear • #4264
Issued: August 31, 1999
Retired: December 23, 1999

Birthdate: January 25, 1999
Castles rise from misty glens
Shielding bands of warrior men
Wearing tartan of their clan
Red, green and a little tan!

Version	Issue Dates	Price Paid	Market Value
Original	Aug. 1999-Dec. 1999		⑤ $33

Page Totals	Price Paid	Market Value

COLLECTOR'S
VALUE GUIDE™

Waves™

Whale · #4084
Issued: May 11, 1997
Retired: May 1, 1998

Birthdate: December 8, 1996
Join him today on the Internet
Don't be afraid to get your feet wet
He taught all the Beanies how to surf
Our web page is his home turf!

231

Version	Issue Dates	Price Paid	Market Value
Original	May 1997-May 1998		⑤ $15 ④ $18

Web™

Spider · #4041
Issued: June 25, 1994
Retired: January 7, 1996

Birthdate: N/A
No Poem

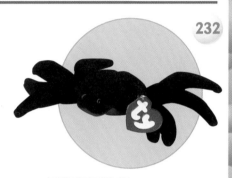

232

Version	Issue Dates	Price Paid	Market Value
Original	June 1994-Jan. 1996		③ $1,100 ② $1,200 ① $1,450

Weenie™

Dachshund · #4013
Issued: January 7, 1996
Retired: May 1, 1998

Birthdate: July 20, 1995
Weenie the dog is quite a sight
Long of body and short of height
He perches himself high on a log
And considers himself to be top dog!

233

Version	Issue Dates	Price Paid	Market Value
Original	Jan. 1996-May 1998		⑤ $27 ④ $29 ③ $100

Page Totals	Price Paid	Market Value

234

Whisper™

Deer • #4194
Issued: May 30, 1998
Retired: December 23, 1999

Birthdate: April 5, 1997
She's very shy as you can see
When she hides behind a tree
With big brown eyes and soft to touch
This little fawn will love you so much!

Version	Issue Dates	Price Paid	Market Value
Original	May 1998-Dec. 1999		$8

235

NEW!

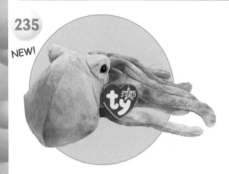

Wiggly™

Octopus • #4275
Issued: February 13, 2000
Current - Just Released

Birthdate: January 25, 2000
Under the sea I travel with ease
I flip and flop – do whatever I please
Being a squid can be lots of fun
Because I swim faster than anyone!

Version	Issue Dates	Price Paid	Market Value
Original	Feb. 2000-Current		$_____

236

Wise™

Owl • #4187
Issued: May 30, 1998
Retired: December 31, 1998

Birthdate: May 31, 1997
Wise is at the head of the class
With A's and B's he'll always pass
He's got his diploma and feels really great
Meet the newest graduate: Class of '98!

Version	Issue Dates	Price Paid	Market Value
Original	May 1998-Dec. 1998		$24

Page Totals	Price Paid	Market Value

COLLECTOR'S
VALUE GUIDE™

Wiser™

Owl · #4238
Issued: April 22, 1999
Retired: August 27, 1999

Birthdate: June 4, 1999
Waking daily to the morning sun
Learning makes school so much fun
Looking great and feeling fine
The newest graduate, "Class of 99!"

Version	Issue Dates	Price Paid	Market Value
Original	Apr. 1999-Aug. 1999		⑤ $22

Wrinkles™

Bulldog · #4103
Issued: June 15, 1996
Retired: September 22, 1998

238

Birthdate: May 1, 1996
This little dog is named Wrinkles
His nose is soft and often crinkles
Likes to climb up on your lap
He's a cheery sort of chap!

Version	Issue Dates	Price Paid	Market Value	
Original	June 1996-Sept. 1998		⑤ $12	④ $14

Zero™

Penguin · #4207
Issued: September 30, 1998
Retired: December 31, 1998

239

Birthdate: January 2, 1998
Penguins love the ice and snow
Playing in weather twenty below
Antarctica is where I love to be
Splashing in the cold, cold sea!

Version	Issue Dates	Price Paid	Market Value
Original	Sept. 1998-Dec. 1998		⑤ $25

	Price Paid	Market Value
Page Totals		

240

Ziggy™

Zebra · #4063
Issued: June 3, 1995
Retired: May 1, 1998

Birthdate: December 24, 1995
Ziggy likes soccer – he's a referee
That way he watches the games for free
The other Beanies don't think it's fair
But Ziggy the Zebra doesn't care!

Version	Issue Dates	Price Paid	Market Value
Original	June 1995-May 1998		⑤ $19 ④ $21
			③ $90

241

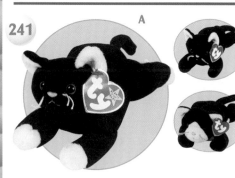

A B C

Zip™

Cat · #4004
Issued: January 7, 1995
Retired: May 1, 1998

Birthdate: March 28, 1994
Keep Zip by your side all the day through
Zip is good luck, you'll see it's true
When you have something you need to do
Zip will always believe in you!

Version	Issue Dates	Price Paid	Market Value
A. White Paws	March 1996-May 1998		⑤ $30 ④ $33
			③ $330
B. All Black	Jan. 1996-Mar. 1996		③ $1,100
C. White Face	Jan. 1995-Jan. 1996		③ $460 ② $540

Page Totals	Price Paid	Market Value

COLLECTOR'S
VALUE GUIDE™

SPORTS PROMOTION BEANIE BABIES®

SPORTS PROMOTION BEANIE BABIES® KEY

Canadian Special Olympics		National Football League		
Major League Baseball		National Hockey League		
National Basketball Association		Women's National Basketball Association		

Beanie Babies giveaways at sporting events have been a major hit with both sports fans and collectors. *Beanies* and sports, it seems, make a winning combination!

1
1999 Signature Bear™
New York Yankees
5/9/99 · N/A
Market Value: $65

2
Baldy™
Philadelphia 76ers
1/17/98 · LE-5,000
Market Value: $90

3
Baldy™
Washington Capitals
2/20/99 · LE-5,000
Market Value: $70

4
Batty™
Milwaukee Brewers
5/31/98 · LE-12,000
Market Value: $50

5
Batty™
New York Mets
7/12/98 · LE-30,000
Market Value: $65

6
Batty™
Seattle Mariners
5/29/99 · LE-15,000
Market Value: $60

7
Blackie™
Boston Bruins
10/12/98 · LE-5,000
Market Value: $65

8
Blackie™
Chicago Bears
In Club Kits · LE-20,000
Market Value: $60

9
Blackie™
Chicago Bears
11/8/98 · LE-8,000
Market Value: $50

10
Blizzard™
Chicago White Sox
7/12/98 · LE-20,000
Market Value: $55

11
Bones™
Chicago Blackhawks
10/24/98 · LE-5,000
Market Value: $67

12
Bones™
New York Yankees
3/10/98 · N/A
Market Value: $90

13
Bongo™
Charlotte Sting
7/17/98 · LE-3,000
Market Value: $100

14
Bongo™
Cleveland Cavaliers
4/5/98 · LE-5,000
Market Value: $75

15
Chip™
Atlanta Braves
8/19/98 · LE-12,000
Market Value: $65

16
Chocolate™
Dallas Cowboys
9/6/98 · LE-10,000
Market Value: $78

17
Chocolate™
Denver Nuggets
4/17/98 · LE-5,000
Market Value: $80

18
Chocolate™
Seattle Mariners
9/5/98 · LE-10,000
Market Value: $55

19
Chocolate™
Tennessee Oilers
10/18/98 · LE-7,500
Market Value: $57

Sports Promotion Beanie Babies*

	Price Paid	Market Value
1.		
2.		
3.		
4.		
5.		
6.		
7.		
8.		
9.		
10.		
11.		
12.		
13.		
14.		
15.		
16.		
17.		
18.		
19.		

Page Totals	Price Paid	Market Value

Sports Promotion Beanie Babies®

20
Chocolate™
Toronto Maple Leafs
1/2/99 · LE-3,000
Market Value: $100

21
Claude™
Sacramento Kings
3/14/99 · LE-5,000
Market Value: $125

22
Cubbie™
Chicago Cubs
1/15-1/17/99 · N/A
Market Value: $350

23
Cubbie™
Chicago Cubs
1/16-1/18/98 · LE-100
Market Value: $385

24
Cubbie™
Chicago Cubs
5/18/97 · LE-10,000
Market Value: $125

25
Cubbie™
Chicago Cubs
9/6/97 · LE-10,000
Market Value: $100

26
Curly™
Charlotte Sting
6/15/98 · LE-5,000
Market Value: $95

27
Curly™
Chicago Bears
12/20/98 · LE-10,000
Market Value: $55

28
Curly™
Cleveland Rockers
8/15/98 · LE-3,200
Market Value: $80

29
Curly™
New York Mets
8/22/98 · LE-30,000
Market Value: $65

30
Curly™
San Antonio Spurs
4/27/98 · LE-2,500
Market Value: $80

31
Daisy™
Chicago Cubs
5/3/98 · LE-10,000
Market Value: $250

Sports Promotion Beanie Babies®	Price Paid	Market Value
20.		
21.		
22.		
23.		
24.		
25.		
26.		
27.		
28.		
29.		
30.		
31.		
32.		
33.		
34.		
35.		
36.		
37.		
38.		
39.		
40.		
41.		
42.		
43.		
44.		
45.		
46.		

32
Derby™
Houston Astros
8/16/98 · LE-15,000
Market Value: $65

33
Derby™
Indianapolis Colts
10/4/98 · LE-10,000
Market Value: $60

34
Dotty™
Los Angeles Sparks
7/31/98 · LE-3,000
Market Value: $70

35
Early™
Milwaukee Brewers
6/12/99 · LE-12,000
Market Value: $40

36
Ears™
Oakland A's
3/15/98 · LE-1,500
Market Value: $90

37
Erin™
Chicago Cubs
8/5/99 · LE-12,000
Market Value: $60

38
Fortune™
Kansas City Royals
6/6/99 · LE-10,000
Market Value: $55

39
Glory™
All-Star Game
7/7/98 · LE-52,000 approx.
Market Value: $150

40
Goatee™
Arizona Diamondbacks
7/8/99 · LE-10,000
Market Value: $50

41
Gobbles™
Phoenix Coyotes
11/26/98 · LE-5,000
Market Value: $60

42
Gobbles™
Phoenix Coyotes
11/26/98 · LE-5,000
Market Value: $60

43
Goochy™
Tampa Bay Devil Rays
4/10/99 · LE-10,000
Market Value: $52

44
Gracie™
Chicago Cubs
9/13/98 · LE-10,000
Market Value: $85

45
Hippie™
Minnesota Twins
6/18/99 · LE-10,000
Market Value: $55

46
Hippie™
St. Louis Blues
3/22/99 · LE-7,500
Market Value: $75

Page Totals	Price Paid	Market Value

COLLECTOR'S VALUE GUIDE™

47
Hissy™
Arizona Diamondbacks
6/14/98 · LE-6,500
Market Value: $60

48
KuKu™
Detroit Tigers
7/11/99 · LE-10,000
Market Value: $50

49
Lucky™
Minnesota Twins
7/31/98 · LE-10,000
Market Value: $55

50
Luke™
Texas Rangers
9/5/99 · LE-15,000
Market Value: $60

51
Mac™
St. Louis Cardinals
6/14/99 · LE-20,000
Market Value: $55

52
Maple™
Canadian Special Olympics
8/97 & 12/97 · N/A
Market Value: $350

53
Mel™
Anaheim Angels
9/6/98 · LE-10,000
Market Value: $60

54
Mel™
Detroit Shock
7/25/98 · LE-5,000
Market Value: $65

55
Millennium™
Chicago Cubs
9/26/99 · LE-40,000
Market Value: $70

56
Millennium™
New York Yankees
8/15/99 · N/A
Market Value: $70

57
Mystic™
Los Angeles Sparks
8/3/98 · LE-5,000
Market Value: $60

58
Mystic™
Washington Mystics
7/11/98 · LE-5,000
Market Value: $85

59
Peace™
Oakland A's
5/1/99 · LE-10,000
Market Value: $65

60
Peanut™
Oakland A's
8/1/98 · LE-15,000
Market Value: $55

61
Peanut™
Oakland A's
9/6/98 · LE-15,000
Market Value: $55

62
Pinky™
San Antonio Spurs
4/29/98 · LE-2,500
Market Value: $70

63
Pinky™
Tampa Bay Devil Rays
8/23/98 · LE-10,000
Market Value: $50

64
Pugsly™
Atlanta Braves
9/2/98 · LE-12,000
Market Value: $50

65
Pugsly™
Texas Rangers
8/4/98 · LE-10,000
Market Value: $52

66
Roam™
Buffalo Sabres
2/19/99 · LE-5,000
Market Value: $55

67
Roary™
Kansas City Royals
5/31/98 · LE-13,000
Market Value: $55

68
Rocket™
Toronto Blue Jays
9/6/98 · LE-12,000
Market Value: $55

69
Rover™
Cincinnati Reds
8/16/98 · LE-15,000
Market Value: $55

70
Sammy™
Chicago Cubs
1/15-1/17/99 · N/A
Market Value: $425

71
Sammy™
Chicago Cubs
4/25/99 · LE-12,000
Market Value: $70

72
Scoop™
Houston Comets
8/6/98 · LE-5,000
Market Value: $80

73
Scorch™
Cincinnati Reds
6/19/99 · LE-10,000
Market Value: $50

Sports Promotion Beanie Babies®		
	Price Paid	Market Value
47.		
48.		
49.		
50.		
51.		
52.		
53.		
54.		
55.		
56.		
57.		
58.		
59.		
60.		
61.		
62.		
63.		
64.		
65.		
66.		
67.		
68.		
69.		
70.		
71.		
72.		
73.		

COLLECTOR'S **VALUE GUIDE**™

Page Totals	Price Paid	Market Value

74
Slippery™
San Francisco Giants
4/11/99 · LE-15,000
Market Value: $50

75
Sly™
Arizona Diamondbacks
8/27/98 · LE-10,000
Market Value: $60

76
Smoochy™
St. Louis Cardinals
8/14/98 · LE-20,000
Market Value: $54

77
Snort™
Chicago Bulls
4/10/99 · LE-5,000
Market Value: $60

78
Spunky™
Buffalo Sabres
10/23/98 · LE-5,000
Market Value: $50

79
Stretch™
New York Yankees
8/9/98 · N/A
Market Value: $55

80
Stretch™
St. Louis Cardinals
5/22/98 · LE-20,000
Market Value: $55

81
Stripes™
Detroit Tigers
5/31/98 · LE-10,000
Market Value: $60

82
Stripes™
Detroit Tigers
8/8/98 · LE-10,000
Market Value: $50

83
Strut™
Indiana Pacers
4/2/98 · LE-5,000
Market Value: $70

84
Tiny™
Houston Astros
7/18/99 · LE-20,000
Market Value: $45

85
Tuffy™
New Jersey Devils
10/24/98 · LE-5,000
Market Value: $65

86
Tuffy™
San Francisco Giants
8/30/98 · LE-10,000
Market Value: $55

87
Valentina™
New York Mets
5/30/99 · LE-18,000
Market Value: $60

88
Valentino™
Canadian Special Olympics
6/98, 9/98 & 10/98 · N/A
Market Value: $190

89
Valentino™
New York Yankees
5/17/98 · LE-10,000
Market Value: $135

90
Waddle™
Pittsburgh Penguins
10/24/98 · LE-7,000
Market Value: $60

91
Waddle™
Pittsburgh Penguins
11/21/98 · LE-7,000
Market Value: $60

92
Waves™
San Diego Padres
8/14/98 · LE-10,000
Market Value: $55

93
Weenie™
Tampa Bay Devil Rays
7/26/98 · LE-15,000
Market Value: $60

94
Whisper™
Milwaukee Bucks
2/28/99 · LE-5,000
Market Value: $50

Sports Promotion Beanie Babies®		
	Price Paid	Market Value
74.		
75.		
76.		
77.		
78.		
79.		
80.		
81.		
82.		
83.		
84.		
85.		
86.		
87.		
88.		
89.		
90.		
91.		
92.		
93.		
94.		
95.		

SPORTS PROMOTION BEANIE BUDDIES®

"Peace" is the first *Beanie Buddy* to be given away at a sporting event.

95
Peace™
Chicago Cubs
4/30/00 · LE-12,000
Market Value: N/E

	Price Paid	Market Value
Page Totals		

COLLECTOR'S
VALUE GUIDE™

Beanie Buddies®

The *Beanie Buddy* line continues to grow in both size and number with the addition of 31 new *Beanie Buddies* in January of 2000. These cuddly critters are even more huggable than ever as some pieces now come in larger sizes: large (22"), extra large (27") and jumbo (48"). Be on the lookout for "Flippity" the blue bunny who is the second *Beanie Buddy* ever to be produced without a corresponding *Beanie Baby* ("Snowboy" was the first). Each current *Beanie Buddy* listed in the Value Guide includes a degree of difficulty rating that indicates how easy or difficult the piece is to find.

2000 Signature Bear™

Bear · #9348
Issued: January 4, 2000
Current - Very Hard To Find

Beanie Buddies® Fact
2000 Ty Signature Bear
Beanie Baby did not exist.
This bear represents the future!

New! ①

Version	Price Paid	Market Value
Original		❷ $_____

Amber™

Cat · #9341
Issued: August 31, 1999
Current - Easy To Find

Beanie Buddies® Fact
Amber and Silver the Beanie Babies were modeled after two orphaned kittens found by Ty Warner!

②

Version	Price Paid	Market Value
Original		❷ $_____
		❶ $20

	Price Paid	Market Value
Page Totals		

133

3

Beak™

Kiwi • #9301
Issued: September 30, 1998
Retired: March 31, 1999

Beanie Buddies® Fact
Beak the Beanie Baby
and Beak the Beanie Buddy
are the first to be released as a set!

Version	Price Paid	Market Value
Original		❶ $47

4

Bongo™

Monkey • #9312
Issued: January 1, 1999
Retired: December 11, 1999

Beanie Buddies® Fact
Bongo the Beanie Baby
was first named Nana.
Ty Warner liked the name Bongo better
because he plays the Bongos!

Version	Price Paid	Market Value
Original		❶ $18

5

Britannia™

(exclusive to the United Kingdom)

Bear • #9601
Issued: August 31, 1999
Current - Impossible To Find

Beanie Buddies® Fact
Britannia the Beanie Baby
was the first international bear
to have an embroidered flag
rather than a patch!

Version	Price Paid	Market Value
Original		❷ $_____
		❶ $150

6

New!

Bronty™

Brontosaurus • #9353
Issued: January 4, 2000
Current - Hard To Find

Beanie Buddies® Fact
Bronty the Beanie Baby was
one of the dinosaur trio. This trio
is highly prized by collectors!

Version	Price Paid	Market Value
Original		❷ $_____

Page Totals	Price Paid	Market Value

COLLECTOR'S
VALUE GUIDE™

Bubbles™

Fish · #9323
Issued: January 1, 1999
Retired: November 29, 1999

Beanie Buddies® Fact
Bubbles the Beanie Baby
made in the swimming position was
quite a challenge to manufacture.

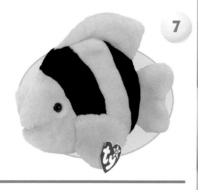

Version	Price Paid	Market Value
Original		❶ $23

Chilly™

Polar Bear · #9317
Issued: January 1, 1999
Retired: November 24, 1999

Beanie Buddies® Fact
Chilly the Beanie Baby
was introduced in June of 1994 and
retired in January of 1996 making
him one of the most sought after!

Version	Price Paid	Market Value
Original		❶ $22

Chip™

Cat · #9318
Issued: January 1, 1999
Retired: December 12, 1999

Beanie Buddies® Fact
Chip the Beanie Baby
due to the variety of colors and pattern shapes,
is one of the most difficult to produce.
It takes over 20 pieces to make Chip!

Version	Price Paid	Market Value
Original		❶ $23

Chocolate™

Moose · #9349
Issued: January 4, 2000
Current - Moderate To Find

New!

Beanie Buddies® Fact
Chocolate the Beanie Baby
was the last of the Original Nine to
be retired!

Version	Price Paid	Market Value
Original		❷ $_____

11

Clubby™ (Club Exclusive)

Bear • #9990
Issued: August 9, 1999
Current - Very Hard To Find

Beanie Buddies® Fact
Clubby the Beanie Baby
was not only the first BBOC Bear,
but also the first to wear a button!

Version	Price Paid	Market Value
Original		❶ $_____

12

Clubby II™ (Club Exclusive)

Bear • #9991
Issued: August 9, 1999
Current – Hard To Find

Beanie Buddies® Fact
Clubby II the Beanie Baby
was the first to be included
in a BBOC Kit!

Version	Price Paid	Market Value
Original		❶ $_____

13

New!

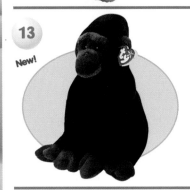

Congo™

Gorilla • #9361
Issued: January 4, 2000
Current - Moderate To Find

Beanie Buddies® Fact
Congo the Beanie Baby was
inspired by the Ty plush gorilla
George!

Version	Price Paid	Market Value
Original		❷ $_____

14

New!

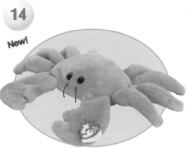

Digger™

Crab • #9351
Issued: January 4, 2000
Current - Hard To Find

Beanie Buddies® Fact
Digger the Beanie Baby
was originally made in orange and
then changed to red!

Version	Price Paid	Market Value
Original		❷ $_____

Page Totals	Price Paid	Market Value

COLLECTOR'S
VALUE GUIDE™

Dotty™

Dalmatian • #9364
Issued: January 4, 2000
Current - Moderate To Find

Beanie Buddies® Fact
Dotty the Beanie Baby was
the second Dalmatian produced by
Ty and still remains a favorite
with collectors!

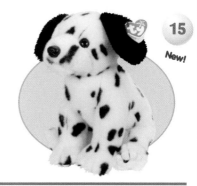

15

New!

Version	Price Paid	Market Value
Original		❷ $_____

Dragon™

Dragon • #9365
Issued: January 4, 2000
Current - Hard To Find

Beanie Buddies® Fact
Scorch the Beanie Baby
was one of the first Beanies to
feature the ty-dyed curly fabric!

16

New!

Version	Price Paid	Market Value
Original		❷ $_____

Erin™

Bear • #9309
Issued: January 1, 1999
Retired: November 19, 1999

Beanie Buddies® Fact
Erin the Beanie Baby
is the first bear to represent a country
but not wear the country's flag!

17

Version	Price Paid	Market Value
Original		❶ $36

Eucalyptus™

Koala Bear • #9363
Issued: January 4, 2000
Current - Moderate To Find

Beanie Buddies® Fact
Eucalyptus the Beanie Baby
was the second koala to be made
by Ty. He was made due to the
popularity of Mel!

18

New!

Version	Price Paid	Market Value
Original		❷ $_____

19 New!

Extra Large Hippie™

Bunny • #9038
Issued: January 4, 2000
Current - Hard To Find

Beanie Buddies® Fact
The length of the ear on the extra
large Hippie is the same length as
the Hippie Buddy!

Version	Price Paid	Market Value
Original		$ ___

20 New!

Extra Large Peace™

Bear • #9036
Issued: January 4, 2000
Current - Hard To Find

Beanie Buddies® Fact
The amount of pellets used to fill
one extra large Buddy can fill 75
Beanie Babies!

Version	Price Paid	Market Value
Original		$ ___

21

Fetch™

Golden Retriever • #9338
Issued: August 31, 1999
Retired: March 10, 2000

Beanie Buddies® Fact
Fetch the Beanie Baby
was introduced in May of 1998 and
retired in December of 1998
when he was less than one year old!

Version	Price Paid	Market Value
Original		② N/E
		① $24

22 New!

Flip™

Cat • #9359
Issued: January 4, 2000
Current - Hard To Find

Beanie Buddies® Fact
Flip the Beanie Baby was
reminiscent of the first item produced
by Ty. A white cat named Kashmir!

Version	Price Paid	Market Value
Original		② $ ___

Page Totals	Price Paid	Market Value

COLLECTOR'S
VALUE GUIDE™

Flippity™

Bunny • #9358
Issued: January 4, 2000
Current - Hard To Find

Beanie Buddies® Fact
Flippity the Beanie Baby
was never made. He is Floppity's
missing twin!

New!

23

Version	Price Paid	Market Value
Original		❷ $_____

Fuzz™

Bear • #9328
Issued: April 1, 1999
Current - Moderate To Find

Beanie Buddies® Fact
Fuzz the Beanie Baby
is made with Tylon that is crimped under
extremely high temperature.

24

Version	Price Paid	Market Value
Original		❷ $_____
		❶ $27

Gobbles™

Turkey • #9333
Issued: August 31, 1999
Retired: December 12, 1999

Beanie Buddies® Fact
Gobbles the Beanie Baby
had several different types of waddles,
including single and double felt!

25

Version	Price Paid	Market Value
Original		❶ $24

Goochy™

Jelly Fish • #9362
Issued: January 4, 2000
Current - Moderate To Find

Beanie Buddies® Fact
Goochy the Beanie Baby's
fabric was one of the most expensive
to produce. The shine on the fabric
makes the ty-dying process more
difficult!

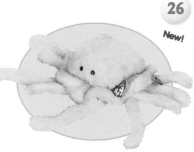

New!

26

Version	Price Paid	Market Value
Original		❷ $_____

Groovy™
Bear • #9345
Issued: January 4, 2000
Current - Very Hard To Find

Beanie Buddies® Fact
Groovy the Beanie Baby
was the first bear to have a colored-
flocked nose!

Version	Price Paid	Market Value
Original		❷ $_____

Halo™
Angel Bear • #9337
Issued: August 31, 1999
Current - Hard To Find

Beanie Buddies® Fact
Halo the Beanie Baby
is made from a special fabric
that shimmers. This fabric
makes Halo even more heavenly!

Version	Price Paid	Market Value
Original		❷ $_____
		❶ $40

Hippie™
Bunny • #9357
Issued: January 4, 2000
Current - Hard To Find

Beanie Buddies® Fact
Hippie the Beanie Baby
was the first bunny to be ty-dyed!

Version	Price Paid	Market Value
Original		❷ $_____

Hippity™
Bunny • #9324
Issued: January 1, 1999
Retired: December 11, 1999

Beanie Buddies® Fact
Hippity the Beanie Baby
is a shade of green called Spring Mint.
This custom color is very difficult
to maintain throughout production.

Version	Price Paid	Market Value
Original		❶ $25

Page Totals	Price Paid	Market Value

COLLECTOR'S
VALUE GUIDE™

Hope™

Bear • #9327
Issued: April 19, 1999
Current - Moderate To Find

Beanie Buddies® Fact
Hope the Beanie Baby
is the first Beanie Baby to be modeled after
one of Ty's plush bears!

Version	Price Paid	Market Value
Original		❷ $_____
		❶ $23

Humphrey™

Camel • #9307
Issued: September 30, 1998
Retired: December 11, 1999

Beanie Buddies® Fact
Humphrey the Beanie Baby
was one of the first to be retired.
Very few were produced,
making him highly collectable!

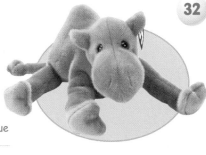

Version	Price Paid	Market Value
Original		❶ $33

Inch™

Inchworm • #9331
Issued: Summer 1999
Retired: January 31, 2000

Beanie Buddies® Fact
Inch the Beanie Baby
was available with both felt
and yarn antennas!

Version	Price Paid	Market Value
Original		❶ $20

Jabber™

Parrot • #9326
Issued: April 16, 1999
Retired: December 12, 1999

Beanie Buddies® Fact
Jabber the Beanie Baby
has 6 colors of fabric and 17 pattern pieces
which make him one of the most difficult
Beanies to produce!

Version	Price Paid	Market Value
Original		❶ $20

35

Jake™

Mallard Duck • #9304
Issued: September 30, 1998
Retired: December 10, 1999

Beanie Buddies® Fact
Jake the Beanie Baby
due to his numerous colors
was difficult to manufacture
making him one of the most sought after!

Version	Price Paid	Market Value
Original		❶ $27

36

New!

Jumbo Peace™

Bear • #9035
Issued: January 4, 2000
Current - Hard To Find

Beanie Buddies® Fact
It takes the same amount of fabric
to produce one jumbo Buddy as it
does to make 25 regular Buddies!

Version	Price Paid	Market Value
Original		❷ $_____

37

New!

Kicks™

Bear • #9343
Issued: January 4, 2000
Current - Hard To Find

Beanie Buddies® Fact
Kicks the Beanie Baby
was the first bear to represent
a sport!

Version	Price Paid	Market Value
Original		❷ $_____

38

New!

Large Fuzz™

Bear • #9040
Issued: January 4, 2000
Current - Hard To Find

Beanie Buddies® Fact
In order for Fuzz to maintain the
proper proportions, longer Tylon
had to be used. The longer the
fur the more difficult it is
to distress!

Version	Price Paid	Market Value
Original		❷ $_____

Page Totals	Price Paid	Market Value

COLLECTOR'S
VALUE GUIDE™

Large Hippie™

Bunny · #9039
Issued: January 4, 2000
Current - Hard To Find

Beanie Buddies® Fact
One large Hippie is the same size
as four Hippie Buddies!

39

New!

Version	Price Paid	Market Value
Original		❷ $_____

Large Peace™

Bear · #9037
Issued: January 4, 2000
Current - Hard To Find

Beanie Buddies® Fact
The larger the Buddy, the longer
the fur and the more difficult
it is to ty-dye the fabric!

40

New!

Version	Price Paid	Market Value
Original		❷ $_____

Lips™

Fish · #9355
Issued: January 4, 2000
Current - Moderate To Find

Beanie Buddies® Fact
Lips the Beanie Baby was one
of the first summer show exclusives.
This makes him very rare and
valuable!

41

New!

Version	Price Paid	Market Value
Original		❷ $_____

Lizzy™

Lizard · #9366
Issued: January 4, 2000
Current - Hard To Find

Beanie Buddies® Fact
Lizzy the Beanie Baby made
with ty-dyed fabric was only produced
for six months, making her one of
the most valuable Beanies!

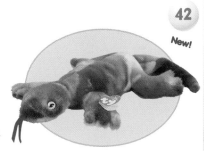

42

New!

Version	Price Paid	Market Value
Original		❷ $_____

43

New!

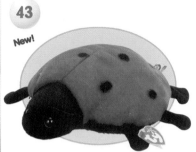

Lucky™

Lady Bug • #9354
Issued: January 4, 2000
Current - Moderate To Find

Beanie Buddies® Fact
Lucky the Beanie Baby
was produced with three varieties of
spots; 7 felt spots, 11 printed spots
and 21 printed spots. Collectors are
very lucky if they have all three!

Version	Price Paid	Market Value
Original		❷ $_____

44

Maple™ (exclusive to Canada)

Bear • #9600
Issued: August 31, 1999
Current - Impossible To Find

Beanie Buddies® Fact
Maple the Beanie Baby
was the first exclusive
international bear!

Version	Price Paid	Market Value
Original		❷ $_____
		❶ $135

45

Millennium™

Bear • #9325
Issued: April 9, 1999
Retired: November 19, 1999

Beanie Buddies® Fact
Millennium the Beanie Baby
commemorates a once in a lifetime event,
making it a once in a lifetime Beanie Baby!

Version	Price Paid	Market Value
Original		❶ $34

46

New!

Nanook™

Husky • #9350
Issued: January 4, 2000
Current - Moderate To Find

Beanie Buddies® Fact
Nanook the Beanie Baby
was the first Beanie to feature
blue eyes rather than black!

Version	Price Paid	Market Value
Original		❷ $_____

Page Totals	Price Paid	Market Value

COLLECTOR'S
VALUE GUIDE™

Osito™ (exclusive to the United States)

Bear · #9344
Issued: January 4, 2000
Current - Hard To Find

Beanie Buddies® Fact
Osito the Beanie Baby
was the first USA exclusive that
did not have a US Flag!

47

New!

Version	Price Paid	Market Value
Original		❷ $_____

Patti™

Platypus · #9320
Issued: January 1, 1999
Retired: July 27, 1999

Beanie Buddies® Fact
Patti the Beanie Baby
was one of the original nine.
Patti was available in both maroon
and magenta!

48

Version	Price Paid	Market Value
Original		❶ $22

Peace™ ♕

Bear · #9335
Issued: August 31, 1999
Current - Very Hard To Find

Beanie Buddies® Fact
Peace the Beanie Baby
was the first Beanie Baby with
an embroidered emblem.
This Ty-dye technique on a soft toy
is the first in the World!

49

Version	Price Paid	Market Value
Original		❷ $_____
		❶ $36

Peanut™

Elephant · #9300
Issued: September 30, 1998
Retired: February 10, 2000

Beanie Buddies® Fact
Peanut the Beanie Baby
made in this royal blue color
is extremely rare and very valuable!

B

A

50

Version	Price Paid	Market Value
A. Royal Blue		❷ $25 ❶ $25
B. Light Blue		❷ $50

51

Peking™
Panda • #9310
Issued: January 1, 1999
Retired: December 10, 1999

Beanie Buddies® Fact
Peking the Beanie Baby
was the first panda made by Ty.
He was retired after only six months
making him highly collectible!

Version	Price Paid	Market Value
Original		❶ $26

52

Pinky™
Flamingo • #9316
Issued: January 1, 1999
Retired: December 12, 1999

Beanie Buddies® Fact
Pinky the Beanie Baby
was a manufacturing challenge
because of her long neck!

Version	Price Paid	Market Value
Original		❶ $18

53

Princess™
Bear • #9329
Issued: April 23, 1999
Current - Very Hard To Find

Beanie Buddies® Fact
N/A

Version	Price Paid	Market Value
Original		❷ $_____
		❶ $42

54

Pumkin'™
Pumpkin • #9332
Issued: August 31, 1999
Retired: November 29, 1999

Beanie Buddies® Fact
Pumkin' the Beanie Baby
was the first Beanie to represent
a vegetable!

Version	Price Paid	Market Value
Original		❶ $27

	Price Paid	Market Value
Page Totals		

COLLECTOR'S
VALUE GUIDE™

Quackers™

Duck · #9302
Issued: September 30, 1998
Retired: July 21, 1999

Beanie Buddies® Fact
Quackers the Beanie Baby
retired in May 1998,
was once made without wings!

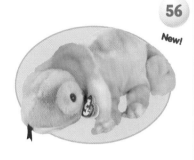

55

Version	Price Paid	Market Value
A. With Wings		❶ $30
B. Without Wing		❶ $250

Rainbow™

Chameleon · #9367
Issued: January 4, 2000
Current - Moderate To Find

Beanie Buddies® Fact
Rainbow the Beanie Baby
and his friend Iggy loved to switch
tags and colors, making them the
most confusing pair to date!

56

New!

Version	Price Paid	Market Value
Original		❷ $_____

Rover™

Dog · #9305
Issued: September 30, 1998
Retired: December 12, 1999

Beanie Buddies® Fact
Rover the Beanie Baby
was the first non-breed dog.
Introduced in the summer of 1996
this red color set him apart!

57

Version	Price Paid	Market Value
Original		❶ $33

Schweetheart™

Orangutan · #9330
Issued: Summer 1999
Retired: January 31, 2000

Beanie Buddies® Fact
Schweetheart the Beanie Baby
has fabric that is tip dyed. It is made with a
special dying process where only the very
tips are dyed a separate color. It is a
very costly and difficult process!

58

Version	Price Paid	Market Value
Original		❶ $20

59

Silver™

Cat · #9340
Issued: August 31, 1999
Current - Easy To Find

Beanie Buddies® Fact
Silver and Amber the Beanie Babies
were modeled after two orphaned
kittens found by Ty Warner!

Version	Price Paid	Market Value
Original		❷ $_____
		❶ $23

60

Slither™

Snake · #9339
Issued: August 31, 1999
Current - Easy To Find

Beanie Buddies® Fact
Slither the Beanie Baby
was the first snake made by Ty.
Since his retirement in 1995
he has learned how to coil!

Version	Price Paid	Market Value
Original		❷ $_____
		❶ $21

61

Smoochy™

Frog · #9315
Issued: January 1, 1999
Retired: November 24, 1999

Beanie Buddies® Fact
Smoochy the Beanie Baby
is the second Beanie Baby frog
made by Ty!

Version	Price Paid	Market Value
Original		❶ $24

62

Snort™

Bull · #9311
Issued: January 1, 1999
Retired: December 12, 1999

Beanie Buddies® Fact
Snort the Beanie Baby
is the second bull made by Ty.
The first bull did not have hooves!

Version	Price Paid	Market Value
Original		❶ $18

Page Totals	Price Paid	Market Value

COLLECTOR'S
VALUE GUIDE™

Snowboy™

63

Snowboy · #9342
Issued: August 31, 1999
Retired: December 12, 1999

Beanie Buddies® Fact
Snowboy the Beanie Baby
was never made. This is the first
and only time this pattern
will be used!

Version	Price Paid	Market Value
Original		❶ $30

Spangle™

64

Bear · #9336
Issued: August 31, 1999
Current - Hard To Find

Beanie Buddies® Fact
Spangle the Beanie Baby
is the first Beanie to feature
two distinct patterned fabrics
and three different head colors!

Version	Price Paid	Market Value
Original		❷ $_____
		❶ $40

Speedy™

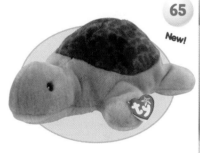

65

New!

Turtle · #9352
Issued: January 4, 2000
Current - Moderate To Find

Beanie Buddies® Fact
Speedy the Beanie Baby
was one of the first Beanie Babies
to feature printed fabric!

Version	Price Paid	Market Value
Original		❷ $_____

Spinner™

66

Spider · #9334
Issued: August 31, 1999
Retired: December 12, 1999

Beanie Buddies® Fact
Spinner the Beanie Baby
was the second spider to be made by Ty.
The attention to detail includes a tiger
striped body and red eyes!

Version	Price Paid	Market Value
Original		❶ $20

	Price Paid	Market Value
Page Totals		

67

Squealer™

Pig • #9313
Issued: January 1, 1999
Retired: November 24, 1999

Beanie Buddies® Fact
Squealer the Beanie Baby
was one of the original nine.
Squealer was so popular that he didn't
retire for over four years!

Version	Price Paid	Market Value
Original		🔹 $20

68

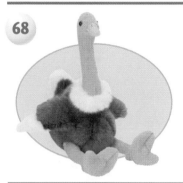

Stretch™

Ostrich • #9303
Issued: September 30, 1998
Retired: December 12, 1999

Beanie Buddies® Fact
Stretch the Beanie Baby
is one of the most difficult to produce
due to her long neck and numerous parts!

Version	Price Paid	Market Value
Original		🔹 $26

69

Teddy™

Bear • #9306
Issued: September 30, 1998
Retired: November 17, 1999

Beanie Buddies® Fact
Teddy the Beanie Baby
was made in six colors.
A very limited number were produced
in this special cranberry color!

Version	Price Paid	Market Value
Original		🔹 $40

70

Tracker™

Basset Hound • #9319
Issued: January 1, 1999
Retired: November 29, 1999

Beanie Buddies® Fact
Tracker the Beanie Baby
has the most expressive eyes.
Close attention to this detail means
limited production.

Version	Price Paid	Market Value
Original		🔹 $21

Page Totals	Price Paid	Market Value

COLLECTOR'S
VALUE GUIDE™

Twigs™

Giraffe • #9308
Issued: September 30, 1998
Retired: January 1, 1999

Beanie Buddies® Fact
Twigs the Beanie Baby
was manufactured in fabric
created exclusively for Ty
and was retired in May 1998!

Version	Price Paid	Market Value
Original		❶ $215

Ty 2K™

71

72

New!

Bear • #9346
Issued: January 4, 2000
Retired: March 8, 2000

Beanie Buddies® Fact
Ty 2K the Beanie Baby's
name was the result of a play
on words with Y2K!

Version	Price Paid	Market Value
Original		❷ N/E

Valentino™

73

New!

Bear • #9347
Issued: January 4, 2000
Current - Hard To Find

Beanie Buddies® Fact
Valentino the Beanie Baby
was the first bear to feature
embroidery!

Version	Price Paid	Market Value
Original		❷ $_____

Waddle™

74

Penguin • #9314
Issued: January 1, 1999
Retired: December 12, 1999

Beanie Buddies® Fact
Waddle the Beanie Baby
was the first of two penguins
to be made by Ty.
He was retired in April of 1998!

Version	Price Paid	Market Value
Original		❶ $20

Beanie Buddies®

75

New!

Weenie™

Dachshund · #9356
Issued: January 4, 2000
Current - Hard To Find

Beanie Buddies® Fact
Weenie the Beanie Baby
was the first Beanie to stand on
all four paws!

Version	Price Paid	Market Value
Original		$_____

76

New!

Zip™

Cat · #9360
Issued: January 4, 2000
Current - Hard To Find

Beanie Buddies® Fact
Zip the Beanie Baby
was made in three styles; all white,
black and white and all black!

Version	Price Paid	Market Value
Original		$_____

Page Totals	Price Paid	Market Value

COLLECTOR'S
VALUE GUIDE™

1997 Teenie Beanie Babies™
Complete Set (set/10)

Issued: April 11, 1997
Retired: May 15, 1997

Version	Price Paid	Market Value
Original		$160

1998 Teenie Beanie Babies™
Complete Set (set/12)

Issued: May 22, 1998
Retired: June 12, 1998

Version	Price Paid	Market Value
Original		$55

1999 Teenie Beanie Babies™
Complete Set (set/12)

Issued: May 21, 1999
Retired: June 3, 1999

Version	Price Paid	Market Value
Original		$40

1999 Teenie Beanie Babies™
International Bears (set/4)

Issued: June 4, 1999
Retired: June 17, 1999

Version	Price Paid	Market Value
Original		$30

Antsy™

Anteater • 3rd Promotion, #2 of 12
Issued: May 21, 1999
Retired: June 3, 1999

Version	Price Paid	Market Value
Original		$5

Bones™

Dog • 2nd Promotion, #9 of 12
Issued: May 22, 1998
Retired: June 12, 1998

Version	Price Paid	Market Value
Original		$7

7

Bongo™

Monkey • 2nd Promotion, #2 of 12
Issued: May 22, 1998
Retired: June 12, 1998

Version	Price Paid	Market Value
Original		$14

8

Britannia™

Bear • 4th Promotion
Issued: June 4, 1999
Retired: June 17, 1999

Version	Price Paid	Market Value
Original		$10

9

Chip™

Cat • 3rd Promotion, #12 of 12
Issued: May 21, 1999
Retired: June 3, 1999

Version	Price Paid	Market Value
Original		$5

10

Chocolate™

Moose • 1st Promotion, #4 of 10
Issued: April 11, 1997
Retired: May 15, 1997

Version	Price Paid	Market Value
Original		$24

11

Chops™

Lamb • 1st Promotion, #3 of 10
Issued: April 11, 1997
Retired: May 15, 1997

Version	Price Paid	Market Value
Original		$28

12

Claude™

Crab • 3rd Promotion, #9 of 12
Issued: May 21, 1999
Retired: June 3, 1999

Version	Price Paid	Market Value
Original		$5

Page Totals	Price Paid	Market Value

COLLECTOR'S
VALUE GUIDE™

Doby™

Doberman • 2nd Promotion, #1 of 12
Issued: May 22, 1998
Retired: June 12, 1998

Version	Price Paid	Market Value
Original		$12

Erin™

Bear • 4th Promotion
Issued: June 4, 1999
Retired: June 17, 1999

Version	Price Paid	Market Value
Original		$10

Freckles™

Leopard • 3rd Promotion, #1 of 12
Issued: May 21, 1999
Retired: June 3, 1999

Version	Price Paid	Market Value
Original		$5

Glory™

Bear • 4th Promotion
Issued: June 4, 1999
Retired: June 17, 1999

Version	Price Paid	Market Value
A. Original		$10
B. McDonald's Employee Bear		$24

Goldie™

Goldfish • 1st Promotion, #5 of 10
Issued: April 11, 1997
Retired: May 15, 1997

Version	Price Paid	Market Value
Original		$20

Happy™

Hippo • 2nd Promotion, #6 of 12
Issued: May 22, 1998
Retired: June 12, 1998

Version	Price Paid	Market Value
Original		$6

Iggy™
Iguana • 3rd Promotion, #6 of 12
Issued: May 21, 1999
Retired: June 3, 1999

Version	Price Paid	Market Value
Original		$5

Inch™
Inchworm • 2nd Promotion, #4 of 12
Issued: May 22, 1998
Retired: June 12, 1998

Version	Price Paid	Market Value
Original		$6

Lizz™
Lizard • 1st Promotion, #10 of 10
Issued: April 11, 1997
Retired: May 15, 1997

Version	Price Paid	Market Value
Original		$15

Maple™
Bear • 4th Promotion
Issued: June 4, 1999
Retired: June 17, 1999

Version	Price Paid	Market Value
Original		$10

Mel™
Koala • 2nd Promotion, #7 of 12
Issued: May 22, 1998
Retired: June 12, 1998

Version	Price Paid	Market Value
Original		$6

'Nook™
Husky • 3rd Promotion, #11 of 12
Issued: May 21, 1999
Retired: June 3, 1999

Version	Price Paid	Market Value
Original		$5

Page Totals	Price Paid	Market Value

Nuts™

Squirrel • 3rd Promotion, #8 of 12
Issued: May 21, 1999
Retired: June 3, 1999

Version	Price Paid	Market Value
Original		$5

25

Patti™

Platypus • 1st Promotion, #1 of 10
Issued: April 11, 1997
Retired: May 15, 1997

Version	Price Paid	Market Value
Original		$30

26

Peanut™

Elephant • 2nd Promotion, #12 of 12
Issued: May 22, 1998
Retired: June 12, 1998

Version	Price Paid	Market Value
Original		$7

27

Pinchers™

Lobster • 2nd Promotion, #5 of 12
Issued: May 22, 1998
Retired: June 12, 1998

Version	Price Paid	Market Value
Original		$6

28

Pinky™

Flamingo • 1st Promotion, #2 of 10
Issued: April 11, 1997
Retired: May 15, 1997

Version	Price Paid	Market Value
Original		$36

29

Quacks™

Duck • 1st Promotion, #9 of 10
Issued: April 11, 1997
Retired: May 15, 1997

Version	Price Paid	Market Value
Original		$16

30

COLLECTOR'S
VALUE GUIDE™

Page Totals	Price Paid	Market Value

31

Rocket™

Blue Jay • 3rd Promotion, #5 of 12
Issued: May 21, 1999
Retired: June 3, 1999

Version	Price Paid	Market Value
Original		$5

32

Scoop™

Pelican • 2nd Promotion, #8 of 12
Issued: May 22, 1998
Retired: June 12, 1998

Version	Price Paid	Market Value
Original		$7

33

Seamore™

Seal • 1st Promotion, #7 of 10
Issued: April 11, 1997
Retired: May 15, 1997

Version	Price Paid	Market Value
Original		$24

34

Smoochy™

Frog • 3rd Promotion, #3 of 12
Issued: May 21, 1999
Retired: June 3, 1999

Version	Price Paid	Market Value
Original		$5

35

Snort™

Bull • 1st Promotion, #8 of 10
Issued: April 11, 1997
Retired: May 15, 1997

Version	Price Paid	Market Value
Original		$17

36

Speedy™

Turtle • 1st Promotion, #6 of 10
Issued: April 11, 1997
Retired: May 15, 1997

Version	Price Paid	Market Value
Original		$20

Page Totals	Price Paid	Market Value

COLLECTOR'S
VALUE GUIDE™

Spunky™

Cocker Spaniel • 3rd Promotion, #4 of 12
Issued: May 21, 1999
Retired: June 3, 1999

Version	Price Paid	Market Value
Original		$5

Stretchy™

Ostrich • 3rd Promotion, #10 of 12
Issued: May 21, 1999
Retired: June 3, 1999

Version	Price Paid	Market Value
Original		$5

Strut™

Rooster • 3rd Promotion, #7 of 12
Issued: May 21, 1999
Retired: June 3, 1999

Version	Price Paid	Market Value
Original		$5

Twigs™

Giraffe • 2nd Promotion, #3 of 12
Issued: May 22, 1998
Retired: June 12, 1998

Version	Price Paid	Market Value
Original		$12

Waddle™

Penguin • 2nd Promotion, #11 of 12
Issued: May 22, 1998
Retired: June 12, 1998

Version	Price Paid	Market Value
Original		$7

Zip™

Cat • 2nd Promotion, #10 of 12
Issued: May 22, 1998
Retired: June 12, 1998

Version	Price Paid	Market Value
Original		$8

BEANIE KIDS™

	Price Paid	Market Value
Page 43		
Page 44		
Page 45		
Page 46		
Page 47		
Subtotals		

BEANIE BABIES®

	Price Paid	Market Value
Page 48		
Page 49		
Page 50		
Page 51		
Page 52		
Page 53		
Page 54		
Page 55		
Page 56		
Page 57		
Page 58		
Page 59		
Page 60		
Subtotals		

BEANIE BABIES™

	Price Paid	Market Value
Page 61		
Page 62		
Page 63		
Page 64		
Page 65		
Page 66		
Page 67		
Page 68		
Page 69		
Page 70		
Page 71		
Page 72		
Page 73		
Page 74		
Page 75		
Page 76		
Page 78		
Page 79		
Page 80		
Page 81		
Page 82		
Subtotals		

BEANIE BABIES™

	Price Paid	Market Value
Page 82		
Page 83		
Page 84		
Page 85		
Page 86		
Page 87		
Page 88		
Page 89		
Page 90		
Page 91		
Page 92		
Page 93		
Page 94		
Page 95		
Page 96		
Page 97		
Page 98		
Page 99		
Page 100		
Page 101		
Page 102		
Subtotals		

	Price Paid	Market Value
Page Totals		

COLLECTOR'S
VALUE GUIDE™

BEANIE BABIES®	Price Paid	Market Value
Page 103		
Page 104		
Page 105		
Page 106		
Page 107		
Page 108		
Page 109		
Page 110		
Page 111		
Page 112		
Page 113		
Page 114		
Page 115		
Page 116		
Page 117		
Page 118		
Page 119		
Page 120		
Page 121		
Page 122		
Page 123		
Subtotals		

BEANIE BABIES™	Price Paid	Market Value
Page 124		
Page 125		
Page 126		
Page 127		
Page 128		
Subtotals		

SPORTS PROMOTION BEANIE BABIES®	Price Paid	Market Value
Page 129		
Page 130		
Page 131		
Page 132		
Subtotals		

BEANIE BUDDIES®	Price Paid	Market Value
Page 133		
Page 134		
Page 135		
Page 136		
Page 137		
Page 138		
Page 139		
Subtotals		

BEANIE BUDDIES®	Price Paid	Market Value
Page 140		
Page 141		
Page 142		
Page 143		
Page 144		
Page 145		
Page 146		
Page 147		
Page 148		
Page 149		
Page 150		
Page 151		
Page 152		
Subtotals		

TEENIE BEANIE BABIES®	Price Paid	Market Value
Page 153		
Page 154		
Page 155		
Page 156		
Page 157		
Page 158		
Page 159		
Subtotals		

COLLECTOR'S VALUE GUIDE™

Grand Totals	Price Paid	Market Value

BEANIE BABIES® & THE SECONDARY MARKET

When voters overwhelmingly voiced their support for continuing the *Beanie Baby* line, the *Beanie Baby* phenomenon proved it had yet to reach its peak and that its dominance would continue into the new millennium. This continued popularity means that you may have to search the secondary market to find the *Beanie Babies* you want.

The secondary market is your source for finding all sorts of plush critters ranging from retired, valuable classics (such as a dark blue "Peanut" *Beanie Baby)* to exclusives never offered to the public (such as a signed "Billionaire bear"). Even if you are just trying to find the 20 new *Beanie Babies*, the secondary market will put you in contact with collectors you never knew existed.

GOING, GOING . . . BUT NOT GONE!

When a *Beanie Baby* retirement is announced, your local Ty retailer is no longer able to order that piece. Newly-retired *Beanies* don't last long on shelves, either, because collectors scramble at their last chance to pick up these retired pieces. But, that doesn't mean these pieces are gone for good!

Talking with your local retailer is a good way to start your secondary market search. Retailers often know of other collectors who may be looking to buy, sell or trade their *Beanies*. This is a good way to learn about other collectors in your area. If local collectors don't have what you are looking for, searching the Internet can put the whole world at your fingertips.

The Internet has become the most vital tool for searching the secondary market. Now you don't have to travel to Germany to nab an elusive "Germania." With the Internet, you can talk to a collector in Germany and have the beloved German exclusive bear in your home in a matter of days. *Beanie*-themed chat rooms and bulletin boards are two good sources for meeting collectors who share your love for *Beanies*. Even if you don't find the piece you are looking for, the friendships you make can be even more rewarding. Remember that common sense should still be followed when talking with strangers on the Internet.

Were you ever afraid of attending an auction because you thought you might stretch your arms and inadvertently bid on a thousand-dollar item? On-line auctions eliminate that fear. There has been a recent explosion in the number of on-line auction sites because now you can bid on exclusive and retired *Beanies* without leaving the comfort of your favorite chair.

BECOME A BEANIE™ EXPERT

Before you make any purchase, it's important to know something about hang tags and tush tags because they play a big role in determining secondary market value. Whether you pay $20 for "Bones" the dog, or ten times that amount, will depend on which generation tag hangs from his ear. *Beanies* with older generation tags are often worth more than identical pieces with newer tags.

Condition is equally important in determining a secondary market value. A *Beanie* in perfect, "mint" condition will be worth more than a well-worn one. Factors that may also raise secondary market value include variations, such as color and design changes. Stay focused in your *Beanie* search or you may become overwhelmed with the dizzying amount of variations available.

When selecting which Internet auction to participate in, you should find out what safeguards are in place to make sure you get the item for the price decided upon. Many auction sites provide a page for buyers to post comments and feedback. Be wary if the seller has been rated poorly or has been negatively commented on by other buyers.

The Internet is not the only secondary market source at your disposal. Collectible shows such as "swap and sells" allow you a first-hand look at the piece you wish to buy. This means you don't have to rely on the sometimes blurry photos found on Internet web sites.

TIME TO SELL THE BEANIES™

There may come a time when you use the secondary market to sell or trade some of your own pieces. Therefore, always keep your *Beanie Babies* looking their best. Tears, rips, discolorations and missing tags will lower the values of your pieces on the secondary market.

The classified section of your newspaper is a good place to spread the word to other local collectors about your pieces for sale. If the classifieds don't produce the desired results, the Internet should be your next destination.

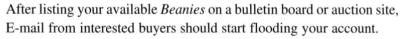

After listing your available *Beanies* on a bulletin board or auction site, E-mail from interested buyers should start flooding your account.

Beanie Babies quickly become members of the family, so even if you don't plan to ever part with them, the secondary market remains instrumental in finding new pieces to welcome into your happy home!

Caring For Your Beanies®

Beanie Babies are well constructed with quality materials in order to withstand the rigors of being loved by a child; however, this does not mean they are indestructible.

THAT BOXED-IN FEELING

For a *Beanie Baby* to be in mint condition, its swing tag and tush tag must be intact and "like new," so it's important not to remove them or write on them. Acrylic tag protectors specifically designed to cover the swing tags may help keep them from becoming ripped or crushed. Similarly, collectors may wish to store individual *Beanies* in acrylic boxes. But if your *Beanies* don't like enclosed spaces, try wrapping them individually in tissue paper and storing them in a plastic storage box with a tight-fitting lid. Many retailers also suggest that you keep your *Beanies* away from direct sunlight, as the ultraviolet rays may cause them to fade.

WASH ME . . . ?

As with any other well-loved stuffed toy, *Beanie Babies* sometimes do get dirty. Just about all *Beanie Babies* and *Beanie Buddies* may be surface cleaned with a washcloth and warm water. Most *Beanie Babies* that are used as toys can also go in the washing machine, but only with an extremely mild detergent. Be sure to remove the swing tag and place the *Beanie* in a sealed pillowcase. And remember, all *Beanies* should all be air dried, not put in the dryer.

If your Beanie needs a little deodorizing and you would rather not put it in the laundry, try placing it in an enclosed container with an opened box of baking soda for about 24 hours.

Beanie™ Variations

Just when collectors think that they have uncovered every possible *Beanie Baby* that exists, another variation pops up to send them scouring the secondary market. Variations have even started turning up among the *Beanie Buddies*. A wingless "Quackers" was the first of the *Buddies* to turn up, and a light blue "Peanut" the elephant is the newest variation to be spotted among the *Buddies*.

COLOR CHANGES

Color changes are often the easiest variations to spot. After all, a tie-dyed "Batty" easily stands out among a crowd of brown ones. "Lizzy" also took a dip in the tie-dye vat, only to later settle on a blue color. "Digger" changed from orange to red, "Happy" switched from gray to lavender and "Patti" achieved a new look when she switched from maroon to magenta. "Peanut" is the most famous of the color change variations. The dark blue versions were produced accidentally and are now worth several thousand dollars more than their light blue counterparts!

DESIGN CHANGES

Design changes can range from subtle ("Derby" and "Mystic" changing from fine to coarse manes) to radical ("old" and "new face" "Teddys"). Seven proved to be an unlucky number for "Lucky" the ladybug. It would later be seen sporting either 11 or 21 spots. "Iggy" and "Rainbow" were originally tight-lipped critters, but they would later be found humorously sticking their tongues out. "Inky" the octopus was even more tight-lipped. He originally had no mouth!

COLLECTOR'S
VALUE GUIDE™

Design changes are not just skin deep. "Princess" comes stuffed with either P.E. (polyethlene) or P.V.C. (polyvinyl chloride) pellets. The tush tag tells which pellets are in your "Princess."

NAME CHANGES

Name changes can fall under two categories: intentional and errors. Some intentional name changes include "Brownie" the bear who had his name changed to the equally appropriate "Cubbie." "Doodle" the rooster also decided to strut his stuff with the new name "Strut." Other name variations are unintentional. "Maple" once wore an incorrect "Pride" tush tag, and "Spinner" has been found with an incorrect "Creepy" tush tag. Whether the change is intentional or not, *Beanie Babies* by any other name are just as cute and cuddly (and collectible)!

Doodle™ style 4171
DATE OF BIRTH : 3 - 8 - 96
Listen closely to "cock-a-doodle-doo"
What's the rooster saying to you?
Hurry, wake up sleepy head
We have lots to do, get out of bed!
Visit our web page!!!
http://www.ty.com

Strut™ style 4171
DATE OF BIRTH : 3 - 8 - 96
Listen closely to "cock-a-doodle-doo"
What's the rooster saying to you?
Hurry, wake up sleepy head
We have lots to do, get out of bed!
Visit our web page!!!
http://www.ty.com

OTHER VARIATIONS

Even something as small as a spelling error can be considered a variation. Swing and tush tags for "Millennium" originally had the bear's name misspelled as "Millenium." Both tags eventually were corrected. "Tuck" and "Spook" might be thought of as name changes, but these are just misspellings for ""Tusk" the walrus and Spooky" the ghost.

Millenium™
DATE OF BIRTH: January 1, 1999
A brand new century has come to call
Health and happiness to one and all
Bring on the fireworks and all the fun
Let's keep the party going 'til 2001 !
www.ty.com

Millennium™
DATE OF BIRTH: January 1, 1999
A brand new century has come to call
Health and happiness to one and all
Bring on the fireworks and all the fun
Let's keep the party going 'til 2001 !
www.ty.com

So keep your eyes sharp the next time you look through the *Beanie Babies* display at your local retail store. You never know – you might find something new among those familiar, smiling faces!

COUNTERFEIT ALERT!

There are two kinds of *Beanie Babies* on the collectible market: genuine ones and fake ones. Whether you're an avid collector or someone who only has a few of the stuffed toys, it's important to know the differences between genuine and counterfeit ones to protect yourself from purchasing an imposter.

INSPECT THE TAGS

Counterfeit

Typically, the easiest way to spot a counterfeit is by inspecting its tags. Swing tags should not have smeared or blurry ink, jagged edges, uneven gold foil around the front of the heart or errors in spelling and punctuation. The generation of the swing tag should be correct. (See page 36 for tag information.) Also, fake tush tags may be wider than the genuine ones.

LOOK AT HOW IT'S MADE

Authentic

Another way to spot a *Beanie* imposter is by looking at how it's made. Genuine *Beanie Babies* are intentionally under-stuffed, so an overstuffed animal or a drastic reduction or absence of pellets should send up caution flags. Fake *Beanie Babies* may have colors that bleed or look dyed, messy stitching, uneven seams or fur that is too shiny or dull. Also, many counterfeits have wrong ribbons and noses that are the wrong colors.

Counterfeit

BECOME INFORMED

Know what genuine *Beanie Babies* look like before purchasing on the secondary market, especially if you do not know the seller. And take your genuine *Beanie Babies* with you to "swap and sells" to use as comparisons. These precautions can help protect your investment, especially if you plan to resell.

BEANIE™ BIRTHDAYS

Many *Beanies* have birth dates that are listed on their swing tags. Do any share a birthday with you? (New releases are listed in red.)

JANUARY

Jan. 1, 1999 - **Millennium™**
Jan. 1, 1999 - **Ty 2K™**
Jan. 1, 2000 - **The Beginning™**
Jan. 2, 1998 - **Zero™**
Jan. 3, 1993 - **Spot™**
Jan. 4, 2000 - **Glow™**
Jan. 5, 1997 - **KuKu™**
Jan. 6, 1993 - **Patti™**
Jan. 8, 1999 - **Tiptoe™**
Jan. 10, 1999 - **Groovy™**
Jan. 13, 1996 - **Crunch™**
Jan. 14, 1997 - **Spunky™**
Jan. 14, 2000 - **Halo II™**
Jan. 15, 1996 - **Mel™**
Jan. 17, 1998 - **Slippery™**
Jan. 18, 1994 - **Bones™**

Jan. 18, 2000 - Scurry™
Jan. 21, 1996 - **Nuts™**
Jan. 23, 1999 - **Schweetheart™**
Jan. 23, 2000 - **Frigid™**
Jan. 24, 2000 - **Swampy™**
Jan. 25, 1995 - **Peanut™**
Jan. 25, 1999 - **Wallace™**
Jan. 25, 2000 - **Wiggly™**
Jan. 26, 1996 - **Chip™**
Jan. 26, 2000 - **Fleecie™**
Jan. 27, 2000 - **Bushy™**

FEBRUARY

Feb. 1, 1996 - **Peace™**
Feb. 1, 2000 - **Niles™**
Feb. 3, 1998 - **Beak™**
Feb. 3, 2000 - **Aurora™**
Feb. 4, 1997 - **Fetch™**
Feb. 5, 1999 - **Osito™**
Feb. 9, 1999 - **Scaly™**
Feb. 10, 2000 - **Grace™**
Feb. 11, 1999 - **Silver™**
Feb. 11, 2000 - **Trumpet™**
Feb. 13, 1995 - **Pinky™**
Feb. 13, 1995 - **Stinky™**
Feb. 14, 1994 - **Valentino™**
Feb. 14, 1998 - **Valentina™**
Feb. 14, 2000 - **Sarge™**
Feb. 17, 1996 - **Baldy™**
Feb. 19, 1998 - **Prickles™**
Feb. 20, 1996 - **Roary™**
Feb. 20, 2000 - **Morrie™**

Feb. 21, 1999 - **Amber™**
Feb. 22, 1995 - **Tank™**
Feb. 22, 2000 - **Sneaky™**
Feb. 23, 1999 - **Paul™**
Feb. 24, 2000 - **Swoop™**
Feb. 25, 1994 - **Happy™**
Feb. 27, 1996 - **Sparky™**
Feb. 28, 1995 - **Flip™**
Feb. 28, 2000 - **Rufus™**
Feb. 29, 2000 - **Springy™**

MARCH

Mar. 1, 1998 - **Ewey™**
Mar. 2, 1995 - **Coral™**
Mar. 2, 1997 - **Curly™** *(Kid)*
Mar. 6, 1994 - **Nip™**
Mar. 8, 1996 - **Doodle™**
Mar. 8, 1996 - **Strut™**
Mar. 9, 1999 - **Clubby II™**
Mar. 10, 1999 - **Swirly™**
Mar. 11, 1999 - **Honks™**
Mar. 12, 1997 - **Rocket™**
Mar. 14, 1994 - **Ally™**
Mar. 15, 1999 - **Lips™**
Mar. 17, 1997 - **Erin™**

Mar. 19, 1996 - **Seaweed™**
Mar. 20, 1997 - **Early™**
Mar. 21, 1996 - **Fleece™**
Mar. 23, 1998 - **Hope™**
Mar. 25, 1999 - **Knuckles™**
Mar. 28, 1994 - **Zip™**
Mar. 29, 1994 - **Angel™** *(Kid)*
Mar. 29, 1998 - **Loosy™**

APRIL

April 1, 1999 - **Neon™**
April 3, 1996 - **Hoppity™**
April 4, 1997 - **Hissy™**
April 5, 1997 - **Whisper™**
April 6, 1998 - **Nibbler™**
April 7, 1997 - **GiGi™**
April 10, 1998 - **Eggbert™**
April 12, 1996 - **Curly™**
April 14, 1999 - **Almond™**
April 15, 1995 - **Rascal™** *(Kid)*
April 15, 1999 - **Pecan™**
April 16, 1997 - **Jake™**

April 18, 1995 - **Ears™**
April 19, 1994 - **Quackers™**
April 21, 1999 - **Chipper™**
April 23, 1993 - **Squealer™**
April 25, 1993 - **Legs™**
April 27, 1993 - **Chocolate™**
April 28, 1999 - **Eucalyptus™**

MAY

May 1, 1995 - **Lucky™**
May 1, 1996 - **Wrinkles™**
May 2, 1996 - **Pugsly™**
May 3, 1996 - **Chops™**
May 4, 1998 - **Hippie™**
May 7, 1998 - **Nibbly™**
May 10, 1994 - **Daisy™**
May 11, 1995 - **Lizzy™**
May 13, 1993 - **Flash™**
May 15, 1993 - **Precious™** *(Kid)*
May 15, 1995 - **Snort™**
May 15, 1995 - **Tabasco™**
May 18, 1999 - **Cheeks™**

May 19, 1995 - **Twigs™**
May 20, 1999 - **Slowpoke™**
May 21, 1994 - **Mystic™**
May 27, 1998 - **Scat™**
May 28, 1996 - **Floppity™**
May 29, 1998 - **Canyon™**
May 30, 1996 - **Rover™**
May 31, 1997 - **Wise™**

JUNE

June 1, 1996 - **Hippity™**
June 2, 1999 - **Flitter™**
June 3, 1996 - **Freckles™**
June 3, 1996 - **Scottie™**
June 4, 1999 - **Wiser™**
June 5, 1997 - **Tracker™**
June 8, 1995 - **Bucky™**
June 8, 1995 - **Manny™**
June 10, 1998 - **Mac™**
June 11, 1995 - **Stripes™**

June 12, 1992 - **Ginger™** *(Kid)*
June 14, 1999 - **Spangle™**
June 15, 1996 - **Scottie™**
June 15, 1998 - **Luke™**
June 16, 1998 - **Stilts™**
June 17, 1996 - **Gracie™**
June 19, 1993 - **Pinchers™**
June 23, 1998 - **Sammy™**
June 27, 1995 - **Bessie™**

JULY

July 1, 1996 - **Maple™**
July 1, 1996 - **Scoop™**
July 2, 1995 - **Bubbles™**
July 4, 1996 - **Lefty™**
July 4, 1996 - **Righty™**
July 4, 1997 - **Glory™**
July 7, 1998 - **Clubby™**
July 8, 1993 - **Splash™**
July 14, 1995 - **Ringo™**

July 15, 1994 - **Blackie™**
July 19, 1995 - **Grunt™**
July 20, 1995 - **Weenie™**
July 20, 1997 - **Chipper™** *(Kid)*
July 23, 1998 - **Fuzz™**
July 28, 1996 - **Freckles™**
July 31, 1998 - **Scorch™**

AUGUST

Aug. 1, 1995 - **Garcia™**
Aug. 1, 1998 - **Mooch™**
Aug. 9, 1995 - **Hoot™**
Aug. 11, 1994 - **Boomer™** *(Kid)*
Aug. 12, 1997 - **Iggy™**
Aug. 13, 1996 - **Spike™**
Aug. 14, 1994 - **Speedy™**

Aug. 16, 1998 - **Kicks™**
Aug. 17, 1995 - **Bongo™**
Aug. 23, 1995 - **Digger™**
Aug. 27, 1995 - **Sting™**
Aug. 28, 1997 - **Pounce™**
Aug. 31, 1998 - **Halo™**

SEPTEMBER

Sept. 3, 1995 - **Inch™**
Sept. 3, 1996 - **Claude™**
Sept. 3, 1996 - **Tumbles™** *(Kid)*
Sept. 5, 1995 - **Magic™**
Sept. 8, 1998 - **Tiny™**
Sept. 9, 1997 - **Bruno™**
Sept. 12, 1996 - **Sly™**
Sept. 16, 1995 - **Derby™**

Sept. 16, 1995 - **Kiwi™**
Sept. 18, 1995 - **Tusk™**
Sept. 21, 1997 - **Stretch™**
Sept. 27, 1998 - **Roam™**
Sept. 29, 1997 - **Stinger™**

OCTOBER

Oct. 1, 1997 - **Smoochy**™
Oct. 2, 1998 - **Butch**™
Oct. 3, 1990 - **Germania**™
Oct. 3, 1996 - **Bernie**™
Oct. 9, 1996 - **Doby**™
Oct. 10, 1997 - **Jabber**™
Oct. 12, 1996 - **Tuffy**™
Oct. 14, 1997 - **Rainbow**™
Oct. 16, 1995 - **Bumble**™
Oct. 17, 1996 - **Dotty**™
Oct. 22, 1996 - **Snip**™

Oct. 28, 1996 - **Spinner**™
Oct. 29, 1996 - **Batty**™
Oct. 30, 1995 - **Radar**™
Oct. 31, 1995 - **Spooky**™
Oct. 31, 1998 - **Pumkin'**™
Oct. 31, 1999 - **Sheets**™

NOVEMBER

Nov. 3, 1997 - **Puffer**™
Nov. 4, 1998 - **Goatee**™
Nov. 6, 1996 - **Pouch**™
Nov. 7, 1997 - **Ants**™
Nov. 9, 1996 - **Congo**™
Nov. 14, 1993 - **Cubbie**™
Nov. 14, 1994 - **Goldie**™
Nov. 18, 1998 - **Goochy**™
Nov. 20, 1997 - **Prance**™
Nov. 21, 1996 - **Nanook**™
Nov. 27, 1996 - **Gobbles**™

Nov. 28, 1995 - **Teddy**™ (brown)
Nov. 29, 1994 - **Inky**™

DECEMBER

Dec. 2, 1996 - **Jolly**™
Dec. 6, 1997 - **Fortune**™
Dec. 6, 1998 - **Santa**™
Dec. 8, 1996 - **Waves**™
Dec. 12, 1996 - **Blizzard**™
Dec. 14, 1996 - **Seamore**™
Dec. 15, 1997 - **Britannia**™
Dec. 16, 1995 - **Velvet**™
Dec. 19, 1995 - **Waddle**™
Dec. 21, 1996 - **Echo**™
Dec. 22, 1996 - **Snowball**™

Dec. 24, 1995 - **Ziggy**™
Dec. 25, 1996 - **1997 Teddy**™
Dec. 25, 1998 - **1998 Holiday
Teddy**™
Dec. 25, 1999 - **1999 Holiday
Teddy**™
Dec. 26, 1996 - **Cutie**™ *(Kid)*

COLLECTOR'S
VALUE GUIDE™

Beanie™ Yearbook

When did your *Beanie Babies* join the collection? This section lists the *Beanie Babies* in order of the year they were issued, and tells you the actual date each one joined its friends in the world of Ty.

January 1994

1/8/94 .... Brownie™/Cubbie™
the bear
1/8/94 .... Chocolate™ the moose
1/8/94 .... Flash™ the dolphin
1/8/94 .... Legs™ the frog
1/8/94 .... Patti™ the platypus
1/8/94 .... Pinchers™ the lobster
1/8/94 .... Splash™ the whale
1/8/94 .... Spot™ the dog
1/8/94 .... Squealer™ the pig

June 1994

6/25/94.... Ally™ the alligator
6/25/94.... Blackie™ the bear
6/25/94 ... Bones™ the dog
6/25/94.... Chilly™ the polar bear
6/25/94.... Daisy™ the cow
6/25/94.... Digger™ the crab
6/25/94.... Goldie™ the goldfish
6/25/94.... Happy™ the hippo
6/25/94.... Humphrey™ the camel
6/25/94.... Inky™ the octopus
6/25/94.... Lucky™ the ladybug
6/25/94.... Mystic™ the unicorn
6/25/94.... Peking™ the panda
6/25/94.... Quackers™ the duck
6/25/94.... Seamore™ the seal

June 1994, cont.

6/25/94.... Slither™ the snake
6/25/94.... Speedy™ the turtle
6/25/94.... Teddy™ (brown)
the bear
6/25/94.... Teddy™ (cranberry)
the bear
6/25/94.... Teddy™ (jade) the bear
6/25/94.... Teddy™ (magenta)
the bear
6/25/94.... Teddy™ (teal) the bear
6/25/94.... Teddy™ (violet)
the bear
6/25/94.... Trap™ the mouse
6/25/94.... Web™ the spider

January 1995

1/7/95 .... Nip™ the cat
1/7/95 .... Valentino™ the bear
1/7/95 .... Zip™ the cat

June 1995

6/3/95 .... Bessie™ the cow
6/3/95 .... Bronty™
the brontosaurus
6/3/95 .... Bubbles™ the fish
6/3/95 .... Bumble™ the bee
6/3/95 .... Caw™ the crow
6/3/95 .... Coral™ the fish

JUNE 1995, CONT.

6/3/95 .... Derby™ the horse
6/3/95 .... Flutter™ the butterfly
6/3/95 .... Inch™ the inchworm
6/3/95 .... Kiwi™ the toucan
6/3/95 .... Lizzy™ the lizard
6/3/95 .... Magic™ the dragon
6/3/95 .... Nana™/Bongo™
      the monkey
6/3/95 .... Peanut™ the elephant
6/3/95 .... Pinky™ the flamingo
6/3/95 .... Rex™ the tyrannosaurus
6/3/95 .... Steg™ the stegosaurus
6/3/95 .... Sting™ the stingray
6/3/95 .... Stinky™ the skunk
est. 6/3/95 .. Stripes™ the tiger
6/3/95 .... Tabasco™ the bull
est. 6/3/95 .. Tusk™ the walrus
6/3/95 .... Velvet™ the panther
6/3/95 .... Waddle™ the penguin
6/3/95 .... Ziggy™ the zebra

SEPTEMBER 1995

9/1/95 .... Radar™ the bat
9/1/95 .... Spooky™ the ghost

JANUARY 1996

1/7/96 .... Bucky™ the beaver
1/7/96 .... Chops™ the lamb
1/7/96 .... Ears™ the rabbit
1/7/96 .... Flip™ the cat
1/7/96 .... Garcia™ the bear
1/7/96 .... Grunt™ the razorback
1/7/96 .... Hoot™ the owl
1/7/96 .... Manny™ the manatee
1/7/96 .... Ringo™ the raccoon

JANUARY 1996, CONT.

1/7/96 .... Seaweed™ the otter
est. 1/7/96 .. Tank™ the armadillo
1/7/96 .... Twigs™ the giraffe
1/7/96 .... Weenie™ the dachshund

JUNE 1996

6/15/96. ... Congo™ the gorilla
6/15/96. ... Curly™ the bear
6/15/96. ... Freckles™ the leopard
6/15/96. ... Lefty™ the donkey
6/15/96. ... Libearty™ the bear
6/15/96. ... Righty™ the elephant
6/15/96. ... Rover™ the dog
6/15/96. ... Scoop™ the pelican
6/15/96. ... Scottie™ the Scottish terrier
6/15/96. ... Sly™ the fox
6/15/96. ... Sparky™ the dalmatian
6/15/96. ... Spike™ the rhinoceros
6/15/96. ... Wrinkles™ the bulldog

JANUARY 1997

1/1/97 .... Bernie™ the St. Bernard
1/1/97 .... Crunch™ the shark
1/1/97 .... Doby™ the Doberman
1/1/97 .... Fleece™ the lamb
1/1/97 .... Floppity™ the bunny
1/1/97 .... Gracie™ the swan

January 1997, cont.

1/1/97 .... Hippity™ the bunny
1/1/97 .... Hoppity™ the bunny
1/1/97 .... Maple™ the bear
1/1/97 .... Mel™ the koala
1/1/97 .... Nuts™ the squirrel
1/1/97 .... Pouch™ the kangaroo
1/1/97 .... Snip™ the Siamese cat
1/1/97 .... Snort™ the bull

May 1997

5/11/97.... Baldy™ the eagle
5/11/97.... Blizzard™ the tiger
5/11/97.... Chip™ the cat
5/11/97.... Claude™ the crab
5/11/97.... Doodle™ the rooster
5/11/97.... Dotty™ the dalmatian
5/11/97.... Echo™ the dolphin
5/11/97.... Jolly™ the walrus
5/11/97.... Nanook™ the husky
5/11/97.... Peace™ the bear
5/11/97.... Pugsly™ the pug dog
5/11/97.... Roary™ the lion
5/11/97.... Tuffy™ the terrier
5/11/97.... Waves™ the whale

July 1997

7/12/97.... Strut™ the rooster

October 1997

10/1/97.... 1997 Teddy™ the bear
10/1/97.... Batty™ the bat
10/1/97.... Gobbles™ the turkey
10/1/97.... Snowball™ the snowman

October 1997, cont.

10/1/97.... Spinner™ the spider
10/29/97... Princess™ the bear

December 1997

12/31/97... Britannia™ the bear
12/31/97... Bruno™ the dog
12/31/97... Hissy™ the snake
12/31/97... Iggy™ the iguana
12/31/97... Pounce™ the cat
12/31/97... Prance™ the cat
12/31/97... Puffer™ the puffin
12/31/97... Rainbow™ the chameleon
12/31/97... Smoochy™ the frog
12/31/97... Spunky™ the cocker spaniel
12/31/97... Stretch™ the ostrich

January 1998

1/31/98.... Erin™ the bear

May 1998

5/1/98 .... Clubby™ the bear
5/30/98.... Ants™ the anteater
5/30/98.... Early™ the robin
5/30/98.... Fetch™
        the golden retriever
5/30/98.... Fortune™ the panda
5/30/98.... GiGi™ the poodle
5/30/98.... Glory™ the bear
5/30/98.... Jabber™ the parrot
5/30/98.... Jake™ the mallard duck
5/30/98.... KuKu™ the cockatoo
5/30/98.... Rocket™ the blue jay

MAY 1998, CONT.

5/30/98. . . . Stinger™ the scorpion
5/30/98. . . . Tracker™ the basset hound
5/30/98. . . . Whisper™ the deer
5/30/98. . . . Wise™ the owl

SEPTEMBER 1998

9/26/98. . . . Billionaire bear™ the bear
9/30/98. . . . 1998 Holiday Teddy™
the bear
9/30/98. . . . Beak™ the kiwi
9/30/98. . . . Canyon™ the cougar
9/30/98. . . . Halo™ the angel bear
9/30/98. . . . Loosy™ the goose
9/30/98. . . . Pumkin'™ the pumpkin
9/30/98. . . . Roam™ the buffalo
9/30/98. . . . Santa™ the elf
9/30/98. . . . Scorch™ the dragon
9/30/98. . . . Zero™ the penguin

DECEMBER 1998

12/12/98. . . #1 Bear™ the bear

JANUARY 1999

1/1/99 . . . . 1999 Signature Bear™
the bear
1/1/99 . . . . Butch™ the bull terrier
1/1/99 . . . . Eggbert™ the chick
1/1/99 . . . . Ewey™ the lamb
1/1/99 . . . . Fuzz™ the bear
1/1/99 . . . . Germania™ the bear
1/1/99 . . . . Goatee™ the mountain goat
1/1/99 . . . . Goochy™ the jellyfish
1/1/99 . . . . Hippie™ the bunny
1/1/99 . . . . Hope™ the bear

JANUARY 1999, CONT.

1/1/99 . . . . Kicks™ the bear
1/1/99 . . . . Luke™ the black lab
1/1/99 . . . . Mac™ the cardinal
1/1/99 . . . . Millennium™ the bear
1/1/99 . . . . Mooch™ the spider monkey
1/1/99 . . . . Nibbler™ the rabbit
1/1/99 . . . . Nibbly™ the rabbit
1/1/99 . . . . Prickles™ the hedgehog
1/1/99 . . . . Sammy™ the bear
1/1/99 . . . . Scat™ the cat
1/1/99 . . . . Slippery™ the seal
1/1/99 . . . . Stilts™ the stork
1/1/99 . . . . Tiny™ the Chihuahua
1/1/99 . . . . Valentina™ the bear

MARCH 1999

3/31/99. . . . Clubby II™ the bear

APRIL 1999

4/8/99 . . . . Eucalyptus™ the koala
4/8/99 . . . . Neon™ the seahorse
4/8/99 . . . . Pecan™ the bear
4/11/99. . . . Schweetheart™
the orangutan
4/12/99. . . . Paul™ the walrus
4/14/99. . . . Knuckles™ the pig
4/14/99. . . . Swirly™ the snail
4/16/99. . . . Tiptoe™ the mouse
4/17/99. . . . Cheeks™ the baboon
4/17/99. . . . Osito™ the bear
4/19/99. . . . Almond™ the bear
4/20/99. . . . Amber™ the cat
4/21/99. . . . Silver™ the cat
4/22/99. . . . Wiser™ the owl
4/24/99. . . . Spangle™ the bear

SUMMER 1999

Summer . . . B.B. Bear™ the bear
Summer . . . Flitter™ the butterfly
Summer . . . Lips™ the fish

SEPTEMBER 1999

9/12/99. . . . Billionaire 2™ the bear

AUGUST 1999

8/31/99. . . . 1999 Holiday Teddy™
the bear
8/31/99. . . . Chipper™ the chipmunk
8/31/99. . . . Groovy™ the bear
8/31/99. . . . Honks™ the goose
8/31/99. . . . Scaly™ the lizard
8/31/99. . . . Sheets™ the ghost
8/31/99. . . . Slowpoke™ the sloth
8/31/99. . . . The End™ the bear
8/31/99. . . . Ty 2K™ the bear
8/31/99. . . . Wallace™ the bear

FEBRUARY 2000

2/13/00. . . . 2000 Signature Bear™
the bear
2/13/00. . . . Aurora™ the polar bear
2/13/00. . . . Bushy™ the lion
2/13/00. . . . Fleecie™ the lamb
2/13/00. . . . Frigid™ the penguin
2/13/00. . . . Glow™ the lightning bug
2/13/00. . . . Grace™ the bunny
2/13/00. . . . Halo II™ the angel bear
2/13/00. . . . Morrie™ the eel
2/13/00. . . . Niles™ the camel
2/13/00. . . . Rufus™ the dog
2/13/00. . . . Sarge™
the German shepherd
2/13/00. . . . Scurry™ the beetle
2/13/00. . . . Sneaky™ the leopard
2/13/00. . . . Springy™ the bunny
2/13/00. . . . Swampy™ the alligator
2/13/00. . . . Swoop™ the pterodactyl
2/13/00. . . . The Beginning™ the bear
2/13/00. . . . Trumpet™ the elephant
2/13/00. . . . Wiggly™ the octopus

COLLECTOR'S CHECKLIST BY TAG GENERATION

CURRENT BEANIE BABIES®

Name	⑥
2000 Signature Bear™	○
Aurora™	○
Bushy™	○
Fleecie™	○
Frigid™	○
Glow™	○
Grace™	○
Halo II™	○
Morrie™	○
Niles™	○
Rufus™	○
Sakura™	○
Sarge™	○
Scurry™	○
Sneaky™	○
Springy™	○
Swampy™	○
Swoop™	○
The Beginning™	○
Trumpet™	○
Wiggly™	○

RETIRED BEANIE BABIES®

Name	①	②	③	④	⑤
#1 Bear™			Special Tag		
1997 Teddy™				○	
1998 Holiday Teddy™					○
1999 Holiday Teddy™					○
1999 Signature Bear™					○
Ally™	○	○	○	○	
Almond™					○
Amber™					○
Ants™					○
B.B. Bear™					○
Baldy™				○	○
Batty™ (tie-dye)					○
Batty™ (brown)				○	□
Beak™					○
Bernie™				○	○
Bessie™			○	○	
Billionaire bear™			Special Tag		
Billionaire 2™			Special Tag		
Blackie™	○	○	○	○	○
Blizzard™				○	○
Bones™	○	○	○	○	○
Bongo™ (tan tail)			○	○	○
Bongo™ (brown tail)			○	○	
Britannia™					○
Bronty™			○		
Brownie™	○				
Bruno™					○
Bubbles™			○	○	
Bucky™			○	○	
Bumble™			○	○	
Butch™					○
Canyon™					○
Caw™			○		
Cheeks™					○
Chilly™	○	○	○		
Chip™				○	○

	1	2	3	4	5
Chipper™					○
Chocolate™	○	○	○	○	○
Chops™			○	○	
Claude™				○	○
Clubby™					○
Clubby II™					○
Congo™				○	○
Coral™			○	○	
Crunch™				○	○
Cubbie™	○	○	○	○	○
Curly™				○	○
Daisy™	○	○	○	○	○
Derby™ (star/fluffy mane)					○
Derby™ (star/coarse mane)					○
Derby™ (no star/coarse mane)				○	○
Derby™ (no star/fine mane)			○		
Digger™ (red)			○	○	
Digger™ (orange)	○	○	○		
Doby™				○	○
Doodle™				○	
Dotty™				○	○
Early™					○
Ears™			○	○	○
Echo™				○	○
Eggbert™					○
Erin™					○
Eucalyptus™					○
Ewey™					○
Fetch™					○
Flash™	○	○	○	○	
Fleece™				○	○
Flip™			○	○	
Flitter™					○
Floppity™				○	○
Flutter™			○		
Fortune™					○
Freckles™				○	○
Fuzz™					○
Garcia™				○	○

	1	2	3	4	5
Germania™					○
GiGi™					○
Glory™					○
Goatee™					○
Gobbles™				○	○
Goldie™	○	○	○	○	○
Goochy™					○
Gracie™				○	○
Groovy™					○
Grunt™			○	○	
Halo™					○
Happy™ (lavender)			○	○	○
Happy™ (gray)	○	○	○		
Hippie™					○
Hippity™				○	○
Hissy™					○
Honks™					○
Hoot™			○	○	
Hope™					○
Hoppity™				○	○
Humphrey™	○	○	○		
Iggy™ (blue/no tongue)					○
Iggy™ (tie-dye/with tongue)					○
Iggy™ (tie-dye/no tongue)					○
Inch™ (yarn antennas)				○	○
Inch™ (felt antennas)			○	○	
Inky™ (pink)			○	○	○
Inky™ (tan/with mouth)			○	○	
Inky™ (tan/without mouth)	○	○			
Jabber™					○
Jake™					○
Jolly™				○	○
Kicks™					○
Kiwi™			○	○	
Knuckles™					○
KuKu™					○
Lefty™				○	
Legs™	○	○	○	○	
Libearty™					○

RETIRED BEANIE BABIES®, cont.

	1	2	3	4	5
Lips™					O
Lizzy™ (blue)			O	O	O
Lizzy™ (tie-dye)			O		
Loosy™					O
Lucky™ (11 spots)				O	O
Lucky™ (21 spots)				O	
Lucky™ (7 spots)	O	O	O		
Luke™					O
Mac™					O
Magic™ (pale pink thread)			O	O	
Magic™ (hot pink thread)				O	
Manny™			O	O	
Maple™ ("Maple™" tush tag)				O	O
Maple™ ("Pride™" tush tag)				O	
Mel™				O	O
Millennium™ ("Millennium™" on both tags)					O
Millennium™ ("Millenium™" swing tag & "Millennium™" tush tag)				❑	
Millennium™ ("Millenium™" on both tags)					O
Mooch™					O
Mystic™ (iridescent horn/fluffy mane)					O
Mystic™ (iridescent horn/coarse mane)				O	O
Mystic™ (brown horn/coarse mane)			O	O	
Mystic™ (brown horn/fine mane)	O	O	O		
Nana™			O		
Nanook™				O	O
Neon™					O
Nibbler™					O
Nibbly™					O
Nip™ (white paws)			O	O	O

RETIRED BEANIE BABIES®, cont.

	1	2	3	4	5
Nip™ (all gold)			O		
Nip™ (white face)		O	O		
Nuts™				O	O
Osito™					O
Patti™ (magenta)			O	O	O
Patti™ (maroon)	O	O	O		
Paul™					O
Peace™				O	O
Peanut™ (light blue)			O	O	O
Peanut™ (dark blue)			O		
Pecan™					O
Peking™	O	O	O		
Pinchers™ ("Pinchers™" swing tag)	O	O	O	O	O
Pinchers™ ("Punchers™" swing tag)	O				
Pinky™			O	O	O
Pouch™				O	O
Pounce™					O
Prance™					O
Prickles™					O
Princess™ (P.E. pellets)				O	
Princess™ (P.V.C. pellets)				O	
Puffer™					O
Pugsly™				O	O
Pumkin'™					O
Quackers™ ("Quackers™"/with wings)		O	O	O	O
Quackers™ ("Quacker™"/without wings)	O	O			
Radar™			O	O	
Rainbow™ (tie-dye/with tongue)					O
Rainbow™ (blue/no tongue)					O
Rex™			O		
Righty™				O	
Ringo™			O	O	O
Roam™					O
Roary™				O	O

	1	2	3	4	5
Rocket™					O
Rover™				O	O
Sammy™					O
Santa™					O
Scaly™					O
Scat™					O
Schweetheart™					O
Scoop™				O	O
Scorch™					O
Scottie™				O	O
Seamore™	O	O	O	O	
Seaweed™			O	O	O
Sheets™					O
Silver™					O
Slippery™					O
Slither™	O	O	O		
Slowpoke™					O
Sly™ (white belly)				O	O
Sly™ (brown belly)				O	
Smoochy™					O
Snip™				O	O
Snort™				O	O
Snowball™				O	
Spangle™ (blue face)					O
Spangle™ (red face)					O
Spangle™ (white face)					O
Sparky™				O	
Speedy™	O	O	O	O	
Spike™				O	O
Spinner™ ("Spinner™" tush tag)				O	O
Spinner™ ("Creepy™" tush tag)					O
Splash™	O	O	O	O	
Spooky™ ("Spooky™" swing tag)		O	O		
Spooky™ ("Spook™" swing tag)		O			
Spot™ (with spot)		O	O	O	
Spot™ (without spot)	O	O			
Spunky™					O

	1	2	3	4	5
Squealer™	O	O	O	O	O
Steg™			O		
Stilts™					O
Sting™			O	O	
Stinger™					O
Stinky™			O	O	O
Stretch™					O
Stripes™ (light w/ fewer stripes)				O	O
Stripes™ (dark w/ fuzzy belly)			O		
Stripes™ (dark w/ more stripes)			O		
Strut™				O	O
Swirly™					O
Tabasco™			O	O	
Tank™ (9 plates/ with shell)				O	
Tank™ (9 plates/ without shell)				O	
Tank™ (7 plates/ without shell)			O		
Teddy™ (brown/new face)			O	O	O
Teddy™ (brown/old face)	O	O			
Teddy™ (cranberry/new face)		O	O		
Teddy™ (cranberry/old face)	O	O			
Teddy™ (jade/new face)		O	O		
Teddy™ (jade/old face)	O	O			
Teddy™ (magenta/new face)		O	O		
Teddy™ (magenta/old face)	O	O			
Teddy™ (teal/new face)		O	O		
Teddy™ (teal/old face)	O	O			

RETIRED BEANIE BABIES®, cont.

	1	2	3	4	5
Teddy™ (violet/new face)		○	○		
Teddy™ (violet/new face/ employee bear with red tush tag)	**No Swing Tag**				
Teddy™ (violet/old face)	○	○			
The End™					○
Tiny™					○
Tiptoe™					○
Tracker™					○
Trap™	○	○	○		
Tuffy™				○	○
Tusk™ ("Tusk™" swing tag)			○	○	
Tusk™ ("Tuck™" swing tag)				○	
Twigs™			○	○	○

RETIRED BEANIE BABIES®, cont.

	1	2	3	4	5
Ty 2K™					○
Valentina™					○
Valentino™		○	○	○	○
Velvet™			○	○	
Waddle™			○	○	
Wallace™					○
Waves™				○	○
Web™	○	○	○		
Weenie™			○	○	○
Whisper™					○
Wise™					○
Wiser™					○
Wrinkles™				○	○
Zero™					○
Ziggy™			○	○	○
Zip™ (white paws)			○	○	○
Zip™ (all black)			○		
Zip™ (white face)		○	○		

CURRENT BEANIE BUDDIES®

	1	2
2000 Signature Bear™		○
Amber™	○	○
Britannia™	○	○
Bronty™		○
Chocolate™		○
Clubby™	○	○
Clubby II™	○	○
Congo™		○
Digger™		○
Dotty™		○
Dragon™		○
Eucalyptus™		○
Extra Large Hippie™	○	
Extra Large Peace™	○	

CURRENT BEANIE BUDDIES®, cont.

	1	2
Flip™		○
Flippity™		○
Fuzz™	○	○
Goochy™		○
Groovy™		○
Halo™	○	○
Hippie™		○
Hope™	○	○
Jumbo Peace™		○
Kicks™		○
Large Fuzz™		○
Large Hippie™		○
Large Peace™		○
Lips™		○
Lizzy™		○

CURRENT BEANIE BUDDIES®, cont.

	1	2
Lucky™		○
Maple™	○	○
Nanook™		○
Osito™		○
Peace™	○	○
Princess™	○	○
Rainbow™		○
Silver™	○	○
Slither™	○	○
Spangle™	○	○
Speedy™		○
Valentino™		○
Weenie™		○
Zip™		○

RETIRED BEANIE BUDDIES®

	❶	❷
Beak™	O	
Bongo™	O	
Bubbles™	O	
Chilly™	O	
Chip™	O	
Erin™	O	
Fetch™	O	O
Gobbles™	O	
Hippity™	O	
Humphrey™	O	
Inch™	O	
Jabber™	O	
Jake™	O	

RETIRED BEANIE BUDDIES®, cont.

	❶	❷
Millennium™	O	
Patti™	O	
Peanut™ (light blue)		O
Peanut™ (dark blue)	O	O
Peking™	O	
Pinky™	O	
Pumkin'™	O	
Quackers™ (with wings)	O	
Quackers™ (without wings)	O	
Rover™	O	
Schweetheart™	O	

RETIRED BEANIE BUDDIES®, cont.

	❶	❷
Smoochy™	O	
Snort™	O	
Snowboy™	O	
Spinner™	O	
Squealer™	O	
Stretch™	O	
Teddy™	O	
Tracker™	O	
Twigs™	O	
Ty 2K™		O
Waddle™	O	

CURRENT BEANIE KIDS™

	❶
Angel™	O
Boomer™	O
Chipper™	O
Curly™	O
Cutie™	O
Ginger™	O
Precious™	O
Rascal™	O
Tumbles™	O

RETIRED TEENIE BEANIE BABIES™

	❶
1997 Teenie Beanie Babies™ Set/12	O
1998 Teenie Beanie Babies™ Set/12	O
1999 Teenie Beanie Babies™ Set/12	O
1999 Teenie Beanie Babies™ International Bears Set/4	O
Antsy™	O
Bones™	O
Bongo™	O
Britannia™	O
Chip™	O
Chocolate™	O
Chops™	O
Claude™	O
Doby™	O
Erin™	O
Freckles™	O
Glory™	O
Glory™ (McDonald's Employee bear)	O
Goldie™	O
Happy™	O

RETIRED TEENIE BEANIE BABIES™, cont.

	❶
Iggy™	O
Inch™	O
Lizz™	O
Maple™	O
Mel™	O
'Nook™	O
Nuts™	O
Patti™	O
Peanut™	O
Pinchers™	O
Pinky™	O
Quacks™	O
Rocket™	O
Scoop™	O
Seamore™	O
Smoochy™	O
Snort™	O
Speedy™	O
Spunky™	O
Stretchy™	O
Strut™	O
Twigs™	O
Waddle™	O
Zip™	O

INDEX BY ANIMAL TYPE

This section offers an easy way to locate your *Beanie Babies*, *Buddies, Kids* and *Teenies* in our Value Guide. Once you find the animal you're looking for, just turn to the page!

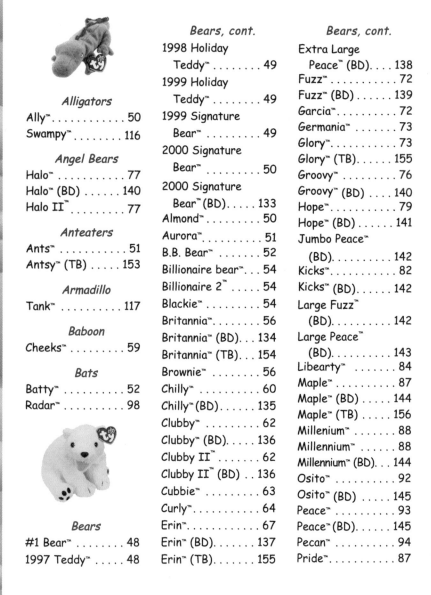

(BD) = Beanie Buddies®

(BK) = Beanie Kids™

(TB) = Teenie Beanie Babies™

ALPHABETICAL INDEX

Below is an alphabetical listing of all the *Beanie Babies*, *Beanie Buddies, Beanie Kids* and *Teenie Beanie Babies*, and the pages on which you can find them in the Value Guide.